MEN OF PATRIOTISM

COURAGE &

ENTERPRISE!

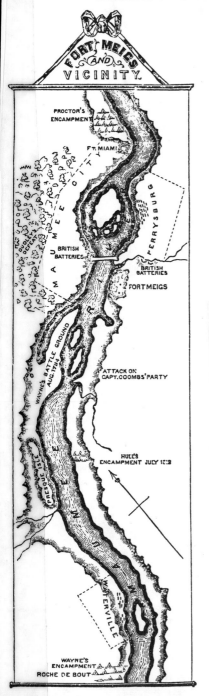

Fort Meigs
in the
War of 1812

D1258636

Larry L. Nelson

A Heritage Classic

Library of Congress Cataloging in Publication Data

Nelson, Larry L.
  Men of patriotism, courage, and enterprise.

  Bibliography: p.
  Includes index.
  1. Fort Meigs (Ohio)--Siege, 1813. I. Title.
E356.M5N44   1985   973.5'23   85-12912

A Facsimile Reprint
Published 1997 by

HERITAGE BOOKS, INC.
1540E Pointer Ridge Place
Bowie, Maryland 20716
1-800-398-7709

ISBN 0-7884-0728-7

A Complete Catalog Listing Hundreds of Titles
On History, Genealogy, and Americana
Available Free Upon Request

For Jackie, Ben, Paul, Rosie and Gracie.

Table of Contents

Acknowledgements

A book of this type is always the result of a cooperative effort from many hands, and I am indebted to many colleagues for their assistance throughout the project. I would like to thank Janet Auten of the English Department, Bowling Green State University, for her careful reading of the original draft. Dennis Au, Associate Director of the Monroe County (Michigan) Historical Society, Professor Randy Buchman, Office of the Vice President, The Defiance College, Brian Dunnigan, Executive Director of Old Fort Niagara and Fellow of the Company of Military Historians, and Michael N. Morell, Curator, Fort Meigs State Memorial, each read subsequent drafts and responded with insightful criticism and direction.

Dr. Amos Loveday, Chief Curator, Education Division, Ohio Historical Society, and Del Harder, Chief, Properties Division, Ohio Historical Society both provided encouragement and guidance throughout the project. The reference librarians wherever I worked proved most helpful, but special thanks should be paid to the staffs at the Ohio Historical Society, The Filson Club, The Burton Historical Collection of the Detroit Public Library, and the Toledo - Lucas County Public Library.

Russ Reinbolt of the Ohio Historical Society typed the original manuscript and then patiently submitted to repeated additions, revisions, and corrections. Lastly, the staff at Fort Meigs State Memorial provided constant comment, stimulation, and enthusiasm. The cooperation and contributions of all who assisted is deeply appreciated.

Preface

This book recounts the history of a small but significant chapter of the Northwest Campaigns of the War of 1812, the story of Fort Meigs from February through September of 1813. The War of 1812 was a conflict of global proportion and international impact. And yet, in a study of this nature it is the human element which reveals itself most clearly. Here we perceive an emotional dimension standing in crisp relief that in studies of a larger scale tends to lose definition and focus. We feel the loneliness and sense the frustration of life in a frontier garrison. We share the terror of a lonely watch on a darkened night; we fear for the safety of comrades. We rejoice in victory and lament in defeat.

In the last analysis it is this human and emotional element, rather than the historical scenario which seems more compelling, more universal, and is part of a world that still clings to warfare as a legitimate instrument of international policy, which is more worthy of our attention.

Where possible, therefore, I have elected to rely on the surviving diaries, letters, and journals of the participants to tell much of the tale, realizing that while occasionally the passage of time may have dulled their memories, the unique perspective that they bring to the events that transpired at the Maumee Rapids remains valid. To this end, where I have quoted from the primary sources, I have done so in the attempt of not only delineating the chronological sequence of events, but also in the hope of shedding light onto the emotional context in which the events took place.

The use of these primary sources, however, often serves to accentuate the underlying and widely held prejudices of the times. The unsympathetic treatment of the Native American is a case in point. Scorn for the Indian runs as a common thread throughout much of the writing of the period, and is inescapably found in some of the excerpts quoted in this work.

For much of white North America during the period, the American Indian was the object of fear and hatred held in equal portion. Utilized by both the government of the United States and that of Great Britain during the war, the tribes of the Indian Nation were, perhaps, the ultimate losers in the conflict. For enemy and ally alike, the dream of Indian autonomy was swept aside by the rush of westward expansion at the war's conclusion. That the Shawnee Chief Tecumseh, who looms large in this story, is universally spoken of as a man of honor, intelligence, and integrity underscores the high esteem in which he was held by both contestants at the Maumee River.

Who, then, were the men who fought at Fort Meigs, and why were they there? In a sense, Lieutenant T. E. Danielson was asking himself much the same question in July of 1812. Danielson was on recruiting duty for the United States Army in Marietta, Ohio at the time. With the war with England but a few days old, his orders were to fill the ranks with able bodied men from the ages of 18 to 45 to serve in the army on the northwest frontier. To encourage the men of Marietta to respond to the call to arms, the Lieutenant published a broadside addressed to "Men of Patriotism, Courage, and Enterprise" for distribution throughout the town.[1] With perception and sensitivity, Danielson had recognized the volatile emotional impact that the declaration of war would engender. His appeal was to those who would express their aspirations with feelings of ardent national pride, personal valor, and hopes of private gain and public recognition.

William Johnson of Delaware County, Ohio also asked himself the same question. Johnson came to Fort Meigs in May of 1813, with a relief column commanded by Brigadier General Green Clay. Participating in an ill-fated assault on the north bank of the Maumee River, he was one of the few of his detachment who, miraculously, managed to escape unharmed to the fort after the disaster.

A self-described "roving blade," Johnson enlisted in the Kentucky Militia in March of 1813, apparently without consulting, or even informing, his wife and family. In April, Johnson found himself on the journey to the Maumee Rapids. With the hardships and tedium of military life taking their toll and the expectation of combat and the possibility of his death weighing heavily on his conscience, he felt compelled to write home and justify his actions.

Most affectionate wife,

> One thing I still think (is) that I am rendering my service in a good cause. I am defending that glorious country and free independent liberty that our forefathers gained by the spilling of their precious blood, more precious than ours, I think, because they were not so numerous as we are, and the enemy, it appears, was more numerous than ours at this time. Just think how our fellow soldiers were treated at Winchester's defeat. I think it is enough to raise the spirits of a dead man almost, if it was possible. Do say that I am a friend to my country, and I am a friend to any man that (is) a friend to his country. And any man that is a foe to his country, I am a foe to that man, because our country is our support and independence. . .[2]

An ordinary man in extraordinary times caught in the rush of political forces that he could neither comprehend nor define, Johnson fought at Fort Meigs because of a fondness for adventure, a thirst for revenge, and an overriding sense of obligation to his country. He and many others had answered the call in their country's time of need out of a deeply seated, though clearly articulated, emotional response.

Altruistic at times, pragmatic at others, the contest for the Maumee Rapids was always a personal one, waged by individuals each with varying degrees of public and private agendas dictating their actions.

The legacy of Fort Meigs is a human one, one of frustration, disappointment, persistance, and accomplishment. The history of Fort Meigs, then, is but a small part of a larger mosaic that ultimately encompassed both hemispheres. Yet the repeated themes recorded by those who fought there ring familiar, forming a rich and complex motif readily identifiable as kindred to the human spirit.

Notes:

[1] T. E. Danielson, "Address to Men of Patriotism, Courage, and Enterprise," July 29, 1812, (Miscel. Broadside Collection, Ohio Historical Society).

[2] "William Johnson to Mary Johnson, April 12, 1813," personal letter (Private collection, photo duplicate and transcription, Fort Meigs collection).

ADDRESS

TO MEN *ATRIOTISM, COURAGE &*
ENTERPRIZE !

Every able bodied man, from the age of 18 to 45 years, who shall be enlisted for the army of the United States, for the term of five years, will be paid, a bounty of sixteen dollars, and five dollars per month ;——and whenever he shall have served the term for which he enlisted, and obtained an honorable discharge, stating that he had faithfully performed his duty, whilst in service, he shall be allowed and paid, in addition to the aforesaid bounty, *three months pay*, and *one hundred & sixty acres of land*——and in case he should be killed in action, or die in the service, his heirs and representatives will be entitled to the said three months pay, and one hundred and sixty acres of land, to be dessignated, surveyed and laid off at the public expence.

To those who prefer enlisting for 18 months, the same pay and bounty will be allowed except the lands.   Apply to

T. E. DANIELSON,

2d Lieut. U. S. Army.

Recruiting Rendezvous,
   Marietta, July 29, 1812.

Men of Patriotism, Courage & Enterprise
Recruiting broadside published in Marietta, Ohio
July 29, 1812, calling for volunteers to serve on the
northwest frontier.

Chapter 1

In the Northwest, the opening strains of the War of 1812 were sounded as early as 1804.[1] Sometime that year Elksawatawa, an obscure Shawnee warrior, received a vision in which he was anointed to organize the Indian Nation against the growing encroachment of the white man. The divine mandate sent to Elksawatawa, or The Prophet, as he came to be known, was fervently embraced by his brother Tecumseh, a war chief of considerable stature among the western tribes. The spiritual imperative supplied by The Prophet, coupled with the demonstrated martial and political prowess of Tecumseh, launched the Indian Nations not only along a path toward cultural revival and redemption, but also along one which led inexorably to increased tension, confrontation, and conflict with the whites.

To implement his brother's vision, Tecumseh set out to organize the western tribes into a confederacy, hoping to accumulate and project a unified Indian political and military resistance against the ever increasing tide of white intrusions into the Indian culture and trespasses onto Indian lands. By 1810, the Confederacy was a reality, centered at Prophet's Town on the banks of the upper Wabash River, at its confluence with the Tippecanoe River in the Indiana Territory.

The relationship between the western Indians and the United

Elksawatawa
Elksawatawa, The Prophet.

States government was, at the time, largely defined by the 1795 Treaty of Greenville, entered into after General Anthony Wayne's victory over the Indians at Fallen Timbers in 1794. The treaty asserted Indian rights to lands north of the Ohio River, though also provided for American territorial perogatives in areas surrounding the United States military outposts in the territory. In 1800, however, William Henry Harrison had become the Governor of the Indiana Territory and had since taking office been vigorously attempting to increase the land holdings of the Territory by negotiating with individual tribes. These tribes, in effect, relinquished their claims to their land in exchange for annual payments of goods and supplies. Harrison's aggressive strategy was successful. By 1809, the terms of these numerous, lesser treaties, which Harrison claimed superceded those dictated in the 1795 agreement, had greatly increased the land available to the Territory's white settlers.

In 1809, Tecumseh, taking advantage of the increasingly unified voice of the fledgling Confederacy, took a vocal and unyielding stand against the legitimacy of Harrison's policies. Protesting that no individual Indian or tribe had the right to bargain away Indian lands without the consent of all Indians, the Shawnee Chief demanded that the Indians who had entered into such a pact with Harrison immediately rescind the agreement, and refuse to accept any further payment of annuities.[2] By the early months of 1810, Indian support for Tecumseh's position, undoubtedly enhanced by his threat to apprehend and kill those unrepentant Indians responsible for entering into the disputed treaties,[3] had grown to the point where Harrison found it necessary to invite the Chief to council.

Held in August, the meeting produced few concrete results. Although Tecumseh demonstrated his ability to marshal an impressive military show of strength by attending with the accompaniment of 400 warriors, he was nonetheless forced to recognize the boundary lines established by the later treaties.[4] Though growing, the strength of the Confederacy was not yet fully realized. For the moment, Tecumseh acquiesced and bided his time.

For Harrison, the council provided the opportunity to assess the personality and abilities of his adversary. The Governor left the meeting both impressed and wary. The prodigious attributes of Tecumseh were not to be lightly dismissed, and by the following autumn Harrison had determined to fortify the Wabash near Prophet's Town.

With the coming of 1811, confrontations between the Indians and whites increased in both frequency and violence. Though Tecumseh was never personally implicated in taking part in any of these raids, Harrison felt that this harrassment was taking place with the implicit encouragement and tacit approval of the Confederacy's leader. Determined to put a stop to the Indian violence, Harrison threatened to attack and destroy all the tribes of the Territory if the raids did not cease. Tecumseh responded by demanding a second council to be held at Vincennes.

The meeting began on July 30, and, as at the first council, Tecumseh arrived with a contingent of about 300 warriors. This time, however, it was Harrison who displayed his military might; and, before the meeting began, he and Tecumseh both watched as over 700 Territorial Militia were paraded and reviewed. The posturing of Harrison notwithstanding, the meeting ended much like the first, with no real agreement and increased animosity between both parties. The sporadic Indian raids continued.[5]

The Federal Government was aware of the deteriorating state of affairs in Indiana, and, in responding to the concerns voiced by the citizens of the Vincennes area, urged Harrison to peacefully resolve the situation. By mid-July, however, the government in Washington had authorized Harrison to take the appropriate military measures if a settlement could not be reached by other means.[6] The Governor, therefore, notified Tecumseh that the tribes of Prophet's Town were to be considered a threat to the area, and their refusal to disperse would lead to their destruction.

Beginning to accumulate and drill an army in late summer and early autumn, Harrison was prepared to march on September 26. Hoping to reach Prophet's Town while Tecumseh was away recruiting in the south, the army moved along the Wabash towards the Indian stronghold stopping long enough to erect two small fortifications, Fort Harrison on the east bank of the Wabash, some 65 miles from Vincennes, and a smaller blockhouse, Fort Boyd, on the west shore below the Vermillion River.

Arriving at the outskirts of Prophet's Town in the afternoon of November 6, the Americans encamped for the night after a mutual agreement with the Indians that there would be no hostilities before a meeting between Harrison and The Prophet could be arranged.[7] Though given no reason to suspect that the Indians would violate their word, Harrison took the precautions that he had followed during the entire march. He ordered that his encampment be fortified, posted a larger than usual guard, deployed his men, and required his soldiers to sleep with their weapons at the ready.

At 4:00 a.m. the following morning, two sentries became alarmed at the sound of movement along the perimeter of the camp. A third guard fired at the noise, and though he was immediately killed by approaching Indians, his shot awakened the sleeping Americans. A surprise Indian assault led by The Prophet was launched against the camp, striking the northwest angle of the encampment and then moving to the left around the position. Only two of the attackers managed to enter the American compound before being cut down, and the American lines held their ground until daylight when charges from both flanks repelled the attack.[8]

The first military confrontation of the War of 1812 in the Northwest, the two hour Battle of Tippecanoe, ended as a decisive victory for Harrison and the Americans. The following day, Prophet's Town, now deserted by the Indians, was burned to the ground. The major military objectives of the campaign were realized. Tecumseh himself, however, by not being present, eluded capture, as did The Prophet, who had managed to escape after the conflict. With Prophet's Town in ruins, the Indians would now, more than ever, openly turn to the British at Fort Malden in Amherstburg, Ontario for support. This explicit connection between the British and Indians would do much the following year to increase the enthusiasm among the whites in the Northwest for a declaration of war with Great Britain.

Indeed, the American victory at Tippecanoe did little to reduce the bitter feelings between the white settlers of the Northwest and the Indians. If anything, the battle had only served to strengthen Tecumseh's resolve in his efforts against the whites. As the Indians drifted toward Fort Malden, the focus of increased tension and concern shifted from Indiana to the Michigan Territory and its capital, Detroit.

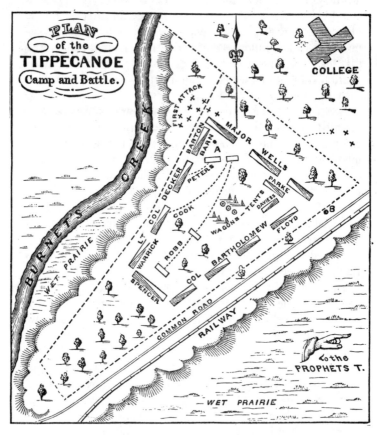

Plan of the Tippecanoe Camp & Battle

The government of the Territory of Michigan was headed by William Hull, a Connecticut native who had served with distinction in the American Revolution. With growing uneasiness, Hull had monitored the events of the previous years, and Harrison's victory on the Wabash had done little to alleviate his fears for the safety of Detroit. In January and February of 1812, the flow of potentially hostile Indians, many of whom had taken part in the Prophet's Town action, into the vicinity, the increasingly deteriorating state of relations with Great Britain, and the growing support for confrontation rather than negotiation among the white inhabitants of the Territory convinced Hull that war with England was imminent. Though war was pending, he had only 173 regular troops at his disposal stationed within the Territory.

Hull had nonetheless taken precautionary steps to strengthen the defensive posture of the Territory. Permission was given to secure recruits for the regular units stationed at Detroit and Michilimackinac. Four companies of Territorial Militia were detached to active duty, and artillery batteries were erected along the Detroit River. Hull realized, however, that despite these steps, Michigan still remained highly vulnerable.

Traveling to Washington in February, Hull met with Secretary of War William Eustis, strongly urging that he be permitted to recruit an army in Ohio for the defense of Michigan and that the United States Government vigorously proceed to build a fleet for the protection of the upper Great Lakes.[9] Though his recommendation concerning the naval fleet was tabled indefinitely for further consideration, Hull left the capital commissioned as a brigadier-general and named as Commanding General of the Army of the Northwest with authorization to call 1,200 men from the Ohio Militia into service for Michigan's defense.[10]

Accumulating supplies and provisions as he returned from Washington to Ohio in mid-May, Hull rendezvoused with his army which had been assembled and organized by Ohio Governor Return Jonathon Meigs in Dayton.[11] On May 25, the Army of the Northwest was paraded and reviewed by both governors.[12] Each man addressed the assembled troops, and Major James Denny of the First Regiment of Ohio Volunteers wrote to his wife that:

William Hull

> when Governor Meigs delivered (his) address, the
> emotions of sympathy which were excited by it can-
> not well be described. Many shed tears. They were
> not tears of regret or sorrow for past events, but
> a burst of manly feelings for the wrongs of their
> beloved country, and then zeal to revenge them.[13]

On June 1, the army began the journey to Detroit, its route
of march taking it nearly due-north through the Great Black
Swamp. The Black Swamp, a vast tract of virtually
uninhabitable land in the northwest corner of Ohio, had been
ceded to the Indians in the Treaty of Greenville. Before Hull
could cross the Indian territory, it was necessary for him to
obtain permission from the appropriate tribes. On June 8,
therefore, a council was held and permission granted for the
army to open a road through the swamp to the Maumee
Rapids. The agreement did not revert ownership of the land
back to the United States, but did permit Hull to build
blockhouses along the route as he proceeded.[14]

The building of the blockhouses through the Black Swamp
was an important element in Hull's strategy, one on which the
safety of the entire army would hinge. With the British Navy
firmly in control of Lake Erie, Detroit's only line of provision
and reinforcement lay overland to the south through the
swamp. Hull's trail and the string of blockhouses that would
be constructed from the southern edge of the Black Swamp
all the way to the Maumee Rapids constituted the virtual life-
line of the army.

Joining with 300 regulars from the 4th Regiment of Infantry, Hull's troops marched as swiftly as the circumstances and
obstacles encountered in the swamp permitted.[15] Several of the
Militia companies, however, became dissatisfied over a delay
in receiving a promised bounty for enlisting. Notices warning
Hull not to continue the march were posted about the encampment, and at morning assembly one militia company refused
to fall into ranks. Hull quickly assembled the members of the
4th Infantry, arrested the officers of the mutinous company,
and summarily court martialed them. Hull, writing of the incident, noted that their sentence was:

to have one half of their heads shaved, their hands tied behind their backs, marched around the lines with a label "Tory" between their shoulders, and drummed out of the Army. After this sentence was published the prisoners appeared remarkably penitent and considered the punishment worse than death itself. Their officers and friends pledged themselves to me for their future good conduct and under all circumstances I consider it expedient to pardon them. Everything now is perfectly quiet, and the army are in high spirits and satisfaction.[16]

Continuing on the march, the army reached the Maumee River and crossed at the Rapids on June 30.

Seeking to speed his journey the following day, Hull hailed the schooner **Cayauga** on the Maumee River and chartered it to continue to Detroit with the sick, the medical supplies, and most of the heavy baggage of the army. Inadvertently, a trunk containing Hull's personal papers and official documents that detailed his troop strength and disposition was placed aboard the vessel as well.[17] Continuing, the army proceeded along the Maumee and encamped for the evening.

In the early hours of July 2, Hull was awakened by an urgent dispatch from Washington. War had been declared on June 18. Incredibly, this critical information had been relayed to Hull through the mail, and only the good fortune of a quick thinking postal employee in Cleveland had prevented further delays in receiving the message. The General at once sent a messenger to intercept the **Cayauga** with a warning, but to no avail. As the schooner moved up the Detroit River under the guns of Fort Malden, the ship was apprehended by the crew of the British brig **General Hunter**. At dawn Hull again resumed the march, pausing briefly at Frenchtown on the River Raisin and then moving cautiously along the Huron River, entering Detroit on July 6, without significant incident.

The situation of the army was not good. Supplies and provisions had not been stored at Detroit in anticipation of the soldier's occupation.[18] The main route of supply, via water, was effectively sealed by the British, and Hull's overland supply line was extremely vulnerable to attack. Over forty pieces of artillery with adequate ammunition were available in the

Detroit area, though not all of these were mounted or in the city. The town's fortification, Fort Detroit, however, was in reasonably good repair.

Hull commanded roughly 2,200 men comprised mostly of Ohio Militia, augmented with small detachments of the Michigan Militia and United States regular troops from the Infantry and Artillery. Though large in number, nearly all of the militia contingent was newly activated, poorly trained and ill disciplined. Furthermore, the Ohio units, in accordance with Ohio law, were commanded by a full colonel, allowing these men in Hull's absence to rank above the lieutenant colonels attached to the units of the regular army. This source of friction, which had caused a few problems while on the march to Detroit, was to continue unabated throughout the campaign.[19]

Hull began to ready Detroit for action at once, ordering that Fort Detroit be strengthened. While attempting to obtain carriages for his dismounted ordnance, he also worked desperately to convince the Indians of the area to remain neutral.[20] Deeply worried for the safety of his supply line through Ohio, he urgently wrote Governor Meigs warning him that the Ohio Militia would have to shoulder the critical responsibility of protecting the overland route.[21]

Given broad authority with which to prosecute the war by Secretary of War Eustis, Hull's strategy was to cross the Detroit River into Sandwich and establish his army there. Though without his full complement of siege artillery he was not strong enough to directly attack and reduce Fort Malden at present, this maneuver would allow the Americans to capture much needed provisions from the British and with the judicious placement of his available artillery, permit some control of the river traffic, all while strengthening the defensive posture of Detroit.[22]

Setting his plan into action on July 12, Hull watched the invasion falter nearly before it began. Several companies of the Ohio Militia refused to cross the river into Canada claiming that the terms of their enlistment in the militia prohibited them from serving on foreign soil. Though most of the recalcitrant men were persuaded to proceed with the attack, the incident only increased the tension between the regular and militia forces. Continuing according to plan, Hull crossed the Detroit River and occupied Sandwich unopposed.

Consolidating his forces and fortifying his position, Hull secured provisions from the surrounding countryside, circulated a proclamation urging the Canadian Militia to join the American cause, and continued to press for Indian neutrality. Though involved in minor skirmishes with the enemy, the American camp, for the moment, remained unmolested by the British.

Although secure at present opposite Detroit, logistical problems, primarily the safety of his overland supply line, continued to plague Hull. A large encampment of Wyandot Indians at Brownstown, setting between Detroit and Frenchtown, had spurned Hull's call for neutrality and had openly allied themselves with the British. Brownstown virtually straddled the American supply line, and the Wyandots there had, since Hull's arrival, become increasingly effective in harassing the army's travel along the road.

In response to Hull's earlier plea for assistance, Governor Meigs advanced all available men forward and had assembled an escort led by Captain Henry Brush of the Ohio Militia to accompany a much needed shipment of supplies and cattle to Detroit. Leaving Chillicothe, Ohio on July 19, the supply train reached the blockhouse at the Maumee Rapids on August 2, and awaited the arrival of reinforcements from Sandusky. Soon joined by two other companies of Ohio Militia, the detachment advanced northward, reaching Frenchtown on August 8.

To aid in the attempt to open his supply route, Hull assembled a 350 man relief force to rendezvous with Brush and accompany him back to Detroit. The relief force from Detroit, commanded by Major Thomas Van Horne, had left the town on August 5. The following morning as the column approached the Brownstown vicinity, the soldiers were met by the deadly fire of an Indian ambush. Caught totally off guard and seemingly surrounded, Van Horne and his men, confused and panic stricken, retreated back to the safety of Detroit.[23]

To open this supply line was critical for the safety of Detroit. Recalling all but a small detachment of troops from Sandwich back to the American side of the Detroit River,[24] Hull mounted another relief expedition of 600 men commanded by Lt. Colonel James Miller of the Infantry. Departing from Detroit on August 9, the force proceeded about 13 miles below the town to the vicinity of the Wyandot village Monguagon. Here it too was surprised by several hundred Indians led by Tecumseh and 400 British soldiers from Fort Malden. This time, however, the American troops held their ground and charges from the infantry and cavalry dispersed the attackers. Though the battle was won, heavy casualties forced Miller to return to Detroit. The supply line remained closed.[25]

Hull quickly notified Brush of Miller's attempt and warned the Militia Captain that the supply line would stay closed unless the relief expedition could approach Detroit by a back route. Brush concurred with Hull's assessment and returned word that he would advance to Godfroy's trading post on the Huron River and await an escort.

Determined to make another attempt at opening the route, Hull ordered Ohio Colonels Duncan McArthur and Lewis Cass to take another detachment of 300 men to the Huron by way of a back trail. Leaving Detroit on August 14, the column reached the Huron without incident. Once at the rendezvous point, however, no sign of Brush and the supply train could be found. Although search details scouted the area, Brush's company could not be located. Dismayed and exasperated, and without adequate provisions to allow them to continue the search, Cass and McArthur gave up the attempt and began the return to Detroit, camping for the night only several miles from the American garrison. Although the information concerning the results of this expedition was of the utmost importance to Hull, the Ohioans made no attempt to contact the General that evening.[26]

At Detroit, Hull's predicament had become a crisis. The British Governor of Upper Canada, Major-General Isaac Brock, had arrived at Fort Malden with a strong detachment of regulars and a force of Indians reported to be 5,000 strong. In addition, Hull had received word that the American post at Mackinac Island had fallen to the enemy.[27] Adding to the internal problems caused by the closed supply line and the general lack of supplies and provisions, a letter highly critical of the General's ability to command had been circulated throughout the American camp.[28] Hull recalled the American troops from Sandwich and consolidated the army within Fort Detroit.

Brock moved swiftly. Crossing to the American shore on August 15, he immediately demanded Hull's surrender. Suggesting that he could not be held responsible for the conduct of the Indians attached to the British army should he be forced to attack, Brock warned that the entire civilian population of Detroit would be placed in great peril should Hull decline.[29]

When he first received the British demands, Hull returned word to Brock that he refused to capitulate, stating that he was prepared to meet any attack that the British might make.[30] In reality, however, the Americans' options were nearly nonexistent. Virtually surrounded by the enemy, cut off from supplies and reinforcements, commanding a large but untrained army, and faced with the possibility of intrigue on the part of his junior officers, Hull could see no chance for victory, and the very real possibility of a wholesale massacre of the town's populace. As the British columns approached Fort Detroit the following morning and formed into battle lines, Hull ordered that the white flag be hoisted above the garrison. Offering no real resistance in his own defense, Hull delivered the Army of the Northwest to the enemy.[31]

Soon after the declaration of war, a call for volunteers was issued in the state of Kentucky. Flushed with the glow of war-fever, over 2,000 men, some from the state's most prominent families, responded to the appeal.[32] Mustered and formally inducted on August 15, at Georgetown, Kentucky, the army was paraded and reviewed the following day, not realizing that at the time of their ceremony the Army of the Northwest had already surrendered to the British.[33]

Leaving for Detroit with William Henry Harrison in command, the army first marched to Newport, Kentucky to receive arms, ammunition, and equipage.[34] Arriving at the arsenal on the Ohio River, the men learned of the fate that had befallen Hull's army. Confused and bitter, the Kentuckians crossed into Ohio and proceeded north to Piqua, arriving there in early September.[35]

On September 5 a large Indian force had laid siege to Fort Wayne, Indiana. Upon receiving word of the battle to their west, the Kentuckians once more fell into formation and marched to the relief of the beleaguered outpost. When news of the approaching column reached the attacking Indians, the siege was lifted, and hostilities had ceased as the reinforcements entered the garrison unchallenged.[36]

HEAD QUARTERS,

PIQUA, September 5, 1812, Four o'Clock, A. M.

MOUNTED VOLUNTEERS!

I requested you in my late address, to rendezvous at Dayton on the 15th inst. I have now a more pressing call for your services. The British and Indians have invaded our country, and are now besieging (perhaps have taken) Fort Wayne. Every friend to his country, who is able so to do, will join me as soon as possible, well mounted, with a good rifle, and twenty or thirty days provision. Ammunition will be furnished at Cincinnati and at Dayton, and the Volunteers will draw provisions (to save their salted meat) at all the public deposits : the Quarter-Masters and Commissaries will see that this order is executed.

WILLIAM HENRY HARRISON.

Call for Mounted Volunteers
Call for mounted volunteers issued by Harrison as he led a column of Kentucky Militia to the relief of Fort Wayne in September, 1812.

The last of the Kentucky forces reached Fort Wayne on September 18, and with them rode Brigadier General James Winchester, recently named to replace Hull as commander of the Northwest Army.[37] Like Hull, Winchester had seen service, as a Captain, during the Revolution, but since then he had remained away from public service. The news of Winchester's appointment was not well received by the men of the Kentucky brigade. Somewhat aloof and lacking the charismatic personality of General Harrison, the soldiers' clear favorite for commander, Winchester nonetheless accepted the responsibilities of his command and secured the fort, ignoring the grumblings of his men.[38] Harrison relinquished command and left Fort Wayne, traveling to St. Mary's where he began to plan for actions that would help secure the western frontier.

Winchester's plan was to advance to Michigan and attempt to retake Detroit before the severe weather of winter halted operations until the following spring. On September 23, Winchester and his army left Fort Wayne, marching down the north bank of the Maumee River towards the ruins of Fort Defiance.[39]

On September 14, a British Force commanded by Major Adam Muir consisting of 150 regulars, 100 Canadian Militia, 800 Indians, and accompanied with three pieces of artillery, had been deployed from Fort Malden to assist the Indians besieging Fort Wayne. On September 25, seven of Muir's Indian scouts had discovered a small advance party of Winchester's men near Defiance and then killed the Americans as the soldiers sat around a campfire. Another patrol of American soldiers discovered their comrade's bodies and briefly engaged the Indian party in a small skirmish. Winchester halted his army at the alarm and erected a defensive earthwork around his camp.

Muir, who was advancing with the main body of the British army along the south shore, realized that the American force could continue to move along the north shore and effectively cut off his retreat to Detroit. Exaggerated reports that detailed the strength of Winchester's army, and the Indians' reluctance to engage a superior force convinced the British commander to abandon the mission. Loading his artillery onto waiting gunboats, Muir and the British army withdrew to Detroit.

Winchester resumed the march. Traveling cautiously because

of the alarm, the army neared the vicinity of Fort Defiance on September 30. Old Fort Defiance had been built over twenty years previously by Anthony Wayne during his campaign against the western tribes. As Winchester approached the long abandoned post he halted the army, began to fortify his position, and awaited instructions and reinforcements. As the encampment was secured, however, the troops with Winchester made their dislike of their commanding officer well known indeed. William Northcutt of the Kentucky Bourbon Blues Light Dragoons recalled that the soldiers:

> . . . all despised him (Winchester), and were continually playing some of their tricks off on him. At one encampment they killed a porcupine and skinned it and stretched the skin over a pole that he used for a particular purpose in the night, and he went and sat down on it, and it like to have ruined him. At another encampment they sawed his pole that he had for the same purpose nearly in two, so that when he went to use it in the night it broke in two and let his Generalship, uniform and all fall backwards in no very decent place, for I seen his Regimentals hanging high upon a pole the next day taking the fresh air.[40]

On the evening of October 2, General Harrison arrived at Defiance to meet with Winchester. Harrison carried news that on September 17, President Madison had given him command of the Army of the Northwest and that Winchester's commission was to be subordinate to his.[41] Winchester's disappointment was matched only by the glee of his troops. In addition, Harrison also brought the plans for a bold strike into Michigan and beyond, the strategy for an offensive which would retake Detroit, repatriate its citizens, and thrust into Upper Canada.

The invasion would involve the movements of three separate arms of the army. From the east, troops of the Virginia and Pennsylvania Militia would converge at Wooster, Ohio and then escort artillery to Upper Sandusky. From there the artillery would be conducted to the Rapids of the Maumee River. In the center, Ohio Militia commanded by General Benjamin Tupper would occupy the supply posts along Hull's Trail and then accumulate supplies and rations for the army. The west or left wing, to be commanded by Winchester, was to provide the offensive man-power to observe, to probe, and to break British resistance along the route. Once assembled and organized, the three wings would converge at the Maumee Rapids in early winter. After the winter freeze forced the British fleet from Lake Erie, the combined army would sweep through Michigan and advance on Canada.[42]

As Harrison left Defiance to take personal charge of the right wing, the task at hand for Winchester was to procure much needed supplies and rations for his army. Though reserves of food and equipment were low, the American General continued his advance, moving his encampment approximately one mile south to the left bank of the Auglaize River, about a mile and a half from its confluence with the Maumee. Once at the site, Winchester ordered that the position be fortified and named Fort Winchester. Built in the form of a parallelogram, Fort Winchester consisted of a log stockade enclosing slightly more than three acres. When completed on October 15, the fort boasted two-story blockhouses constructed at each corner, and an underground passageway that led from a cellar in the post's interior to the Auglaize River.

With Fort Winchester completed, a small detachment was selected to man the post and the remainder of the army ordered to continue the march to the Maumee Rapids. Winchester first advanced to about a mile and a half below the mouth of the Auglaize on the north shore of the Maumee. A lack of firewood at this site, coupled with its low, marshy ground, however, forced the Americans to abandon the site and move to a dryer location two miles further down the river. The second location, too, proved unsatisfactory, and the army again relocated some two miles below the site of the second camp. Here Winchester remained for nearly eight weeks.

Though at long last securely encamped, shortages of provisions and supplies had reached critical dimensions. Dependent, as was the entire United States military establishment at the time, on private contractors for the purchase and delivery of provisions and equipment, Winchester found this notoriously inefficient source of supply woefully inadequate for the needs of his troops. The location of the encampment at Defiance was accessible from the south only by means of a lengthy trip west

to Fort Wayne and then down the Maumee River, or by an
exhausting journey through the perilous Black Swamp. The army, in addition to being the largest of the three wings envi-
sioned by Harrison, was also the one presently closest to the
enemy. With enormous supply requirements, isolated, and
vulnerable to attack, Winchester could find few, if any, contractors willing to assume the risk and mount the effort
necessary to provision his men.[43]

Winchester's troops suffered greatly. Having left Kentucky
in mid-summer, none of the soldiers had been issued winter
clothing. Indeed, some of the troops had not even drawn
shoes.[44] Equally as critical was the shortage of food. The rations carried by the army were quickly being consumed, but
not being replaced. Some of the men subsisted by eating boiled
hickory roots, and Winchester's encampment soon came to be
called "Fort Starvation" by his soldiers. Not surprisingly, given
the conditions of the encampment, an outbreak of typhus swept
through the camp adding to the misery of the men.[45]

While the troops of the left wing languished along the banks
of the Maumee River, the right wing composed of Pennsylvania
and Virginia Militia was organized and began its journey to
Ohio. To the members of the Petersburg Volunteers, a
volunteer company raised in Petersburg, Virginia, the advance
to the Maumee began as a frolic. As Winchester's men starved
in the bitter cold of the Black Swamp, the Petersburg
Volunteers were beginning the march singing "The Girl I Left
Behind Me," traveling northward through Virginia
unhampered by the moderate temperatures of the southern
winter.

Frequently met by an appreciative populace as it passed
through towns along the route, the column was enthusiastically
provided with toasts and feasts held in its honor. As the
volunteer company neared Monticello, a private of the company recalled that:

> We drew up in military array at the base of the hill
> on which the great house was erected. About half
> way down the hill stood a very homely old man,
> dressed in plain Virginia cloth, his head uncovered,
> and his venerable locks flowing in the wind. Some
> of our quizzical clique at once marked him as a fit

subject of fun. "I wonder," said one, "what old codger that is, with his hair blowing nine ways for Easter Monday." "Why of course," said another, "it is the overseer, and he seems to be scared out of a year's growth. I suspect he never saw gentlemen volunteers before." But how we were astonished when he advanced to our officers and introduced himself as THOMAS JEFFERSON! The officers were invited in to a collation, while we were marched off to the town, where more abundant provisions had been made.[46]

Crossing into Ohio at Mount Pleasant, the column continued to Chillicothe where the State General Assembly provided another fete, complete with "fowls and turkeys, pies, tarts, custards, and sweetmeats, and floating islands, and all the luxurious variety that the generous daughters of the Buckeye State could devise."[47]

As the Virginia troops left the hospitality of Chillicothe behind, however, the harsh realities of the Ohio winter, short rations, and poor roads quickly stripped away whatever naive veneer that the company attached to the nature of the mission. Traveling by way of Franklinton and Delaware, the Virginians reached Lower Sandusky cold, exhausted, and sustained by "bread which was sometimes made of damaged flour (that) was truly disgusting."[48]

While the right wing moved northward to rendezvous with the left at the Rapids, Winchester's situation along the Maumee was steadily worsening. By December 16, virtually all of the rations at the encampment were exhausted, and Winchester's men threatened to mutiny if provisions were not secured at once. Fortunately, the following day 300 hogs were driven into camp, and in the days that followed flour, clothing, and other supplies arrived at the encampment with increasing regularity. At long last Winchester was supplied adequately enough to move on the Maumee Rapids in accordance with Harrison's orders. With no small sense of relief the army left Defiance on December 31, arriving at the Rapids on January 13.

The British claimed control of the Rapids, though at the time of Winchester's advance the position was only nominally occupied by a small number of Indians. The Indians quickly fled without offering resistance as the Americans approached, carrying a warning to the commander of Fort Malden, Colonel Henry Proctor. For Proctor, the American movement to the Rapids came as no real surprise. An American attempt to retake Michigan and Detroit had long been anticipated, and indeed was regarded as inevitable. Having only a few regulars at his disposal, the British officer nonetheless began to marshal his troops, call out the militia, and notify his Indian allies.

Food was nowhere abundant on the northwest frontier during the winter of 1812 - 1813. It was, however, available at Frenchtown. Throughout the previous months, the town's inhabitants had powerlessly watched as British forces confiscated much of their stockpiled grain, flour, and livestock. The American advance was seen in the French community as the opportunity to throw off the yoke of British control.[49] Discreetly, messengers were sent from the town to Winchester warning him of the British intentions to fortify the village and urging him to push on to the Raisin and liberate the village.[50]

To Winchester, the availability of provisions at Frenchtown was a powerful argument to advance. Although recently resupplied, the army was, at best, only minimumly provisioned. In addition, the terms of enlistment for many of his men were nearly expired.[51] If he did not move quickly, there would be little chance to neutralize the growing threat of British opposition in the vicinity. At a meeting of his senior officers on the night of the 16th, Winchester decided to ignore his orders to remain at the Rapids, electing instead to push on to Frenchtown.

Notifying Harrison of his decision the following day,[52] Winchester assembled nine companies totalling 554 men for the initial assault. After drawing ammunition and flints for their muskets, the expedition moved over the ice of the Maumee to Lake Erie. From the lake the column would enter Michigan several miles south of the mouth of the River Raisin and then proceed to Frenchtown. Shortly after the column had left the Rapids, Winchester assembled an additional 113 men and sent them to reinforce the first detachment with additional supplies and equipment. Regrouping shortly thereafter at Presque Isle at the western end of the Maumee Bay, the Americans proceeded, approaching the vicinity of the River Raisin settlement in the early afternoon of January 18.

Proctor had been able to marshal and deploy only a small number of his troops in time to meet the Kentuckians' advance, and defending the village at present was only a small detachment of Canadian Militia numbering less than 75 men. A few British regulars joined their ranks along with a lone three pound cannon. Upwards of 200 Potawatomi Indians reinforced the British defenders. To their front lay the Raisin, on the flanks and to the rear a picket fence offered slight protection. The British and Indians watched as the Kentuckians neared, and as the American line came within range they began the engagement with a round of canister from the three pound field piece.

The round missed its mark, flying above the heads of the Americans, but as the Kentucky troops quickly dressed into battle formation, a second round struck home inflicting casualties among the attackers. Still the Americans advanced, preceded by over one hundred of the town's French civilians who had taken up arms to expel the British from their homes. Outnumbered and overwhelmed, the British put up only a brief resistance before beginning an orderly retreat. Using the Indians to provide a covering fire, the cannon would be loaded, fired, and withdrawn a short distance to be loaded and fired again.

The press of the Americans, however, was too great. Though challenging Winchester's men virtually every step of the way while in town, the British finally gave up the fight and retreated to Brownstown twenty miles away, leaving the Kentuckians in possession of the village. The cost to the Americans, though, had been high. Fifty-five of Winchester's men were wounded; twelve lay dead.[53] As the expedition secured the town, word was immediately sent to Winchester notifying him of the victory and urging him to quickly advance with reinforcements.[54]

Leaving only 300 men at the Rapids to guard the army's baggage, Winchester brought the remainder of his troops forward to the Raisin the following day, arriving at Frenchtown in the early hours of January 20. Spending the day touring the site and assessing the deployment of his troops, the American commander realized that his defensive position was inadequate to meet a determined British counter-attack, an event that Winchester and his officers regarded as certain to occur.

The main body of troops which had taken part in the battle

of the 18th occupied the camp which had been established by the British and was protected only by the picket fence. The newly arrived reinforcements were encamped in an open field to the right, in some cases as far as 430 yards distant from the main body of troops. Winchester himself had occupied the home of Colonel Francois Navarre, Frenchtown's most prominent citizen. Though undoubtedly the most lavish accomodations available in the French settlement, Navarre's residence was on the south bank of the Raisin, opposite the location of the army's encampment and nearly a mile upstream from the rest of the Americans. To strengthen the position of the army, it was decided to build a defensive breastwork above the encampment on the north side of the river.[55] Construction, however, was not started because the necessary tools and equipment had not accompanied the troops from the Maumee.[56]

Early on the evening of the 21st, Winchester sent a dispatch to Harrison advising him of the situation and requesting that an additional 1,000 to 1,200 men be forwarded to the Raisin. Though somewhat wary, Winchester was not particularly concerned for the safety of his army despite numerous reports that warned of an impending counter-strike by the British. Without issuing special instructions to his troops, without posting a larger than usual guard, and without sending patrols to scout the perimeter, the American general retired for the evening.[57]

Word of the American victory had been immediately relayed back to Colonel Proctor at Fort Malden. Having missed his opportunity to seriously oppose the Kentuckians as they had first entered Michigan, the British commander was determined to crush the American advance before it could threaten Detroit. Calling out virtually every available regular, militia company, and Indian in the vicinity, Proctor amassed an army in excess of 1,300 strong accompanied by three 3 pound cannons and three small calibre howitzers.

Travelling silently southward, the British force arrived above Frenchtown in the early hours of January 22. Incredibly, the army advanced to within an eighth of a mile of the American lines without being detected. Proctor deployed his men, established his artillery batteries, and waited for dawn to launch the assault.

At first light an American sentry glanced up and noticed the British troops drawn into battle ranks. Quickly taking aim, his

Navarre Cabin
Home of Francois Navarre. Winchester used the
Navarre residence as his headquarters during the
American occupation of Frenchtown in January,
1813.

shot killed a British soldier and alerted the awakening camp. The guard's shot was answered by volleys from the enemy's field pieces and a lethal rain of musket fire from the Canadians and Indians.

For nearly twenty minutes the Kentuckians held their ground as best they could. Strong pressure, though, was brought to bear on the right wing of the encampment, and slowly their line gave way. Falling back, the defenders attempted to regroup with reinforcements at the river, but the confusion caused by the maneuver gained momentum and spread throughout the ranks. What had started as a slight retreat became a rout, and soon over 400 of the Americans were running, every man for himself, in an effort to avoid the advancing enemy onslaught. Among those swept up in the retreat was Winchester. Of the retreating Americans, only a few would escape. Winchester and others were captured; many were killed.

As the right wing disintegrated, the left wing behind the picket fence stood firm. Responding to British advances on their position with devastating musket volleys, the Americans continued to keep the enemy at bay. Three times the British lines approached the puncheon embrasure, each time withering in the face of determined fire from the Kentucky soldiers. At ten in the morning the British temporarily withdrew, leaving the left wing securely emplaced.

Proctor now turned to his captive Winchester and demanded that the General surrender the remaining Americans. When Winchester refused, Proctor, like Brock before him had done at Detroit, replied that he had the means to seize the town by force, but in such an event he could not restrain his Indian allies, and as a result the town's civilian population might suffer the consequences. As a surrendered commander, Winchester still refused to comply, but he did offer to send a letter to Major George Madison, commander of the American left, urging him to surrender.

When Madison received Winchester's letter under a flag of truce, he was shocked beyond words. His position was still strong and he had but few casualties. Though stunned at Winchester's request, the letter forced him to critically reflect upon his situation. Ammunition was already in short supply, and the British forces previously involved in the action on the right could now be brought to bear on the left. Lastly, Proctor's

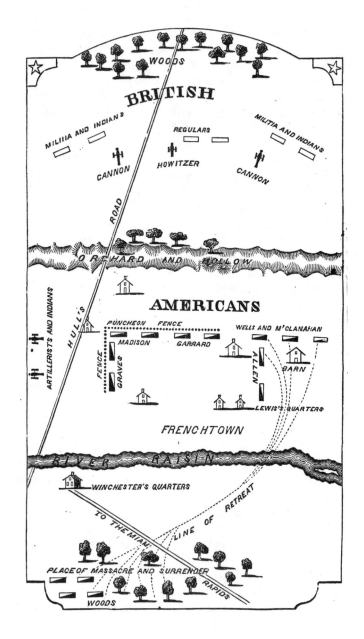

Plan of the Battle of Frenchtown

threats against the Frenchtown noncombatants were not to be lightly dismissed. Clearly Winchester's suggestion to surrender was the correct course to take.[58]

Madison, however, had the presence of mind to negotiate before capitulating. Meeting with Proctor, Madison demanded protection from the Indians for the wounded Americans left in town and the promise that they would be safely escorted to Fort Malden. Proctor agreed. The surrender was accomplished.[59]

Almost immediately after the battle's end, Proctor received word that General Harrison was less than eight miles away accompanied by a large force of additional Americans. Though incorrect, the information had a terrifying effect on the British commander. The American defense of Frenchtown had mauled his army. With many casualties and in a highly vulnerable situation, he was in no position to make a stand. Hastily gathering his army and collecting those American prisoners healthy enough to make the journey to Fort Malden, Proctor began the return to Detroit, leaving with such speed that some wounded British soldiers still remained on the field where they had fallen. Though the wounded Americans had been promised protection as one of the terms of their surrender, only a token guard was left as most of the British army left the field. The injured Kentuckians who were unable to accompany their captors were abandoned to the Indians.

Early the following morning the Indians began to congregate in the village near the homes where the wounded were being billeted. Beginning to move from house to house, the Indians would enter and ransack the dwelling, occasionally molesting the wounded. Before long, one of the Kentuckians was killed. Quickly the violence escalated and a torrent of bloodshed was unleashed as the Indians raged through the town. At times the Americans would be dragged from the houses to be tomahawked in the street; at others the houses would simply be burned with the wounded inside. A British officer who had stood horrified witnessing the scene later wrote that:

> The fierce glare of the flames, the crashing of the
> roofs, the shrieking of the dying wretches enveloped
> in fire and the savage triumphant yelling of these
> monsters in human shape presented so dreadful a

Winchester Humiliated
*Satirical print published in London in May of 1813,
showing a humiliated James Winchester after his capture at the River Raisin being presented to an amused
Henry Proctor.*

MASSACRE of the AMERICAN PRISONERS, at FRENCH-TOWN, on the River Raisin, by the SAVAGES
Under the Command of the British Gen.l PROCTOR : January 23.d 1813.

River Raisin Massacre
Circulated in 1813, this particularly gruesome depiction of the River Raisin Massacre following Winchester's defeat at Frenchtown served to inflame public opinion and strengthen support for the war effort along the northwest frontier.

scene as to beggar the most florid description.[60]

Before the carnage was finished, upwards of sixty Americans had been massacred.[61]

The bloody conclusion of the Battle of the River Raisin marked the end of a disastrous chapter in the Northwest Campaigns. Twice in the seven months since the declaration of war, the United States had seen the Army of the Northwest destroyed. Like the burning buildings of Frenchtown, Harrison's opportunity for a winter invasion of Canada lay in ruins.

Notes for Chapter I

[1] Robert B. McAfee, **History of the Late War in the Western Country**, (Bowling Green: Historical Publications Company, 1919), p. 18.

[2] Ibid., p. 20.

[3] Benson J. Lossing, **The Pictorial Fieldbook of the War of 1812**, (Somersworth: New Hampshire Publishing Company, 1976), p. 190.

[4] McAfee, **History of the Late War**, p. 21.

[5] Ibid., pp. 24-25; Lossing, **Fieldbook**, p. 193.

[6] McAfee, **History of the Late War**, p. 27.

[7] Ibid., p. 35; Lossing, **Fieldbook**, p. 201.

[8] McAfee, **History of the Late War**, pp. 39-43; Lossing, **Fieldbook**, pp. 203-06.

[9] Richard C. Knopf, ed., **Document Transcriptions of The War of 1812 In The Northwest**, Vol 6, pt. 1, **Letters To The Secretary of War 1812 Relating To The War of 1812 In The Northwest**, (Columbus: Ohio Historical Society, 1959), "Hull to Eustis, March 6, 1812," pp. 78-80.

[10] Lossing, **Fieldbook**, p. 201.

[11] Ibid., p. 252; McAfee, **History of the Late War**, p. 62.

[12] Knopf, **Letters To The Secretary of War 1812**, pt. 1, "Hull to Eustis, May 26, 1812," p. 242.

[13] "James Denny to Isabella Denny," personal letter, May 27, 1812, (James Denny Papers, Archives-Library Collection, Ohio Historical Society); see also Lossing, **Fieldbook**, p. 255.

[14] McAfee, **History of the Late War**, p. 64; Knopf, **Letters To The Secretary of War 1812**, pt. 2, "An Agreement Between Hull and the Indians, July 8, 1812," p. 22.

[15] Knopf, **Letters To The Secretary of War 1812**, pt. 2, "Hull to Eustis, June 9, 1812," pp. 26-27.

[16] Ibid., "Hull to Eustis, June 18, 1812," pp. 48-49.

[17] Ibid., "Hull to Eustis, July 3, 1812," p. 76; "Extract of a letter from a Gentleman at Detroit to his friend in this place dated 7th July, 1812," pp. 81-82; "Hull to Eustis, July 7, 1812," p. 85. See also, McAfee, **History of the Late War**, p. 69.

[18] Knopf, **Letters To The Secretary of War 1812**, pt. 2, "Hull to Eustis, July 10, 1812," p. 89; "Hull to Eustis, July 10, 1812," p. 90.

[19] Ibid., "Miller to Eustis, June 12, 1812," p. 33; "Hull to Eustis, June 13, 1812," p. 34; "McArthur et. al. to Hull, July 18, 1812," pp. 105-06; "Hull to Eustis, July 19, 1812," p. 110; "Worthington to Eustis, July 19, 1812," p. 115.

[20] Ibid., "Hull to Eustis, July 7, 1812," p. 85.

[21] Ibid., "Hull to Meigs, July 19, 1812," p. 141.

[22] Ibid., "Hull to Eustis, July 9, 1812," p. 88.

[23] McAfee, **History of the Late War**, pp. 87-88; Lossing, **Fieldbook**, p. 276.

[24] Knopf, **Letters To The Secretary of War 1812**, pt. 3, "Hull to Eustis, August 8, 1812," p. 16.

[25] Lossing, **Fieldbook**, pp. 279-82; McAfee, **History of the Late War**, pp. 90-94.

[26] McAfee, **History of the Late War**, pp. 98-99.

[27] Knopf, **Letters To The Secretary of War 1812**, pt. 3, "Hanks to Hull, August 4, 1812," pp. 6-7.

[28] Lossing, **Fieldbook**, pp. 282-83.

[29] Ibid., p. 286; McAfee, **History of the Late War**, pp. 98-99.

[30] Lossing, **Fieldbook**, p. 286; McAfee, **History of the Late War**, p. 100.

[31] McAfee, **History of the Late War**, p. 104.

[32] Ibid., p. 118.

[33] Ibid., p. 120.

[34] Knopf, **Letters To The Secretary of War 1812**, pt. 3, "Clay to Eustis, August 22, 1812," p. 53.

[35] McAfee, **History of the Late War**, p. 137.

[36] Ibid., pp. 137-43.

[37] Knopf, **Letters To The Secretary of War 1812**, pt. 3, "Adams to Eustis, September 19, 1812," p. 164.

[38] McAfee, **History of the Late War**, p. 148.

[39] Knopf, **Letters To The Secretary of War 1812**, pt. 3, "Winchester to Eustis, September 22, 1812," p. 184.

[40] Glen J. Clift, "War of 1812 Diary of William B. Northcutt," **Kentucky Historical Society Register** 56 (1958) : p. 176.

[41] McAfee, **History of the late War**, p. 165.

[42] Lossing, **Fieldbook**, p. 329.

[43] Ibid., pp. 348-49.

[44] Knopf, **Letters To The Secretary of War 1812**, pt. 4, "Winchester to Eustis, November 20, 1812," p. 110.

[45] McAfee, **History of the Late War**, pp. 202-05.

[46] Alfred M. Lorrain, **The Helm, The Sword, And The Cross: A Life Narrative**, (Cincinnati: Poe & Hitchcok, 1862), pp. 103-04.

[47] Ibid. p. 106. Chillicothe served as Ohio's Capital from 1803-10, and from 1812-16.

[48] Ibid., p. 109.

[49] Lossing, **Fieldbook**, p. 352.

[50] McAfee, **History of the Late War**, p. 223.

[51] Lossing, **Fieldbook**, p. 351.

[52] Richard C. Knopf, ed., **Document Transcriptions of The War of 1812 In The Northwest**, Vol. 7, pt. 1, **Letters To The Secretary of War 1813 Relating To The War of 1812 In The Northwest**, (Columbus: Ohio Historical Society, 1961), "Winchester to Harrison, January 17, 1813," p. 36.

[53] McAfee, **History of the Late War**, pp. 225-53.

[54] Knopf, **Letters To The Secretary of War 1813**, pt. 1, "Lewis to Winchester, January 20, 1813," pp. 42-43; also Lossing, **Fieldbook**, pp. 352-53.

[55] Lossing, **Fieldbook**, pp. 352-53.

[56] Knopf, **Letters To The Secretary of War 1813**, pt. 1, "Winchester to Harrison, January 21, 1813," p. 49.

[57] Lossing, **Fieldbook**, p. 354.

[58] Richard C. Knopf, ed., **Document Transcriptions of The War of 1812 In The Northwest**, Vol. 5, pt. 2, **The National Intelligencer Reports The War of 1812 In The Northwest**, (Columbus: Ohio Historical Society, 1958), "Winchester to The Secretary of War, January 23, 1813," p. 29.

[59] Lossing, **Fieldbook**, p. 357.

[60] [Major Peter Chambers?], "The War in Canada 1812 - 1814," Public Archives of Canada, MB40-0-1B.

[61] Lossing, **Fieldbook**, p. 358; Knopf, **The National Intelligencer Reports**, pt. 2, "Gen. Winchester's Army, from the **Pittsburgh Mercury** of February 25," pp. 33-37; "Deposition of Gustavus M. Bower, April 24, 1813," pp. 220-21; "John Todd, M.D. to the Hon. Jesse Bledsoe, May 2, 1813," pp. 222-24; McAfee, **History of the Late War**, pp. 231-42.

Chapter 2

General Harrison was advancing with the leading contingent of the right wing of the army to a point north of the Maumee River Rapids when he first received news of the River Raisin defeat during the evening hours of the 22nd. The early reports were verified by Major Elijah McClenahan of the Kentucky Volunteer Militia. McClenahan, the ranking officer who had managed to escape after the Frenchtown action, related that the British forces consisted of from 1,600 to 2,000 British and Indians, heavily reinforced by field artillery and howitzers.[1] Harrison now had to determine whether the British would continue their thrust and engage him at his present position, and if this was the case, whether the 900 men with him, strengthened only with a single piece of artillery, could effectively resist the attack.

Calling a council of his general and field officers that night, Harrison, with McClenahan present, reviewed the events which had transpired and sought advice on how to proceed.[2] The council's recommendation was unanimous. Harrison's present position was untenable. Even though the enemy might advance with only a portion of the force at its disposal, it was possible for them to circumvent Harrison's position to the south and attack his supply lines from Sandusky, separating the army from much needed provisions and reinforcements. The council at first considered re-establishing the army at a fortification erected by Winchester at the Maumee Rapids, on the north side of the river near the site of Wayne's Fallen Timbers battle ground. This idea was rejected as well. The existing fort, built on the opposite side of the Maumee from the source of Harrison's supplies, would be difficult to provision should heavy rains cause the river to rise. In addition, the enclosure had been constructed in such a manner as to make it highly vulnerable to a concerted attack. It was agreed, then, that Harrison should withdraw to a point south of the Maumee and join with the troops and artillery following him under the command of Brigadier General Joel Leftwich of the Virginia Militia. Then, after consolidating his forces, he could renew the invasion of Canada.[3]

Harrison acted quickly. At dawn of the following morning, the troops began the retreat. Stopping at Winchester's fortification, Harrison ordered that it be burned to the ground. The fort contained a large quantity of grain and supplies, but Harrison had no means of transporting these provisions and ordered them destroyed as well. Once Winchester's works were reduced, Harrison continued the withdrawal, re-crossing the Maumee and proceeding to a point on the Portage River some 18 miles south of the Rapids. Arriving at the Portage, the army pitched camp and awaited the arrival of Leftwich.

Harrison did not yet realize that the British had elected not to pursue the Americans after the Frenchtown battle. While he continued to fear for the safety of his troops, rain and mud had become the real adversary. Unseasonably warm weather and generous rains had rendered the route to the Portage a quagmire. Dangerously extended over miles of nearly impassable roads, the remainder of Harrison's army trickled into the encampment. On January 24, Greenbury Keen, a Sergeant in the First Regiment, Second Brigade of the Pennsylvania Militia, enroute to the Portage, recorded:

> We continued our march and found the roads much worse than they were the last ten miles. We frequently were obliged to wade through ponds mid-leg deep for one mile at a time. We arrived in camp about 4 o'clock p.m. Our baggage did not come on. We had no camp equipage, and borrowed some

axes and made fires. We cut brush for bedding, and
wet and weary lay ourselves down to rest.[4]

On the 27th, Harrison ordered that the arms and ammunition of the assembled troops be inspected. Many of the cartridges that had been issued to the men were discovered to have
been damaged by the rain, and these were replaced. Calling
a meeting of his senior officers at his quarters that evening,
Harrison gave specific instructions as to how each was to conduct his command in case of attack. Each soldier was ordered
to sleep with his musket in his arms and his cartridge box under
his head. The watch-word for the evening guard was issued,
and it too reflected Harrison's concern that an attack was imminent, "Fight On!"[5]

On January 30, Leftwich arrived at the Portage with the remainder of the troops under his command, accompanied by
Captain Daniel Cushing's Company of the 2nd Regiment of
the Artillery. Harrison now had at his disposal an effective
force of approximately 1,700 men, reinforced by the reassur-
ing presence of five 18 pound cannons, six 6 pounders and three
howitzers. However, the rain that had begun on the 24th and
which had hampered the assemblage of the troops at the Portage continued, preventing Harrison from advancing.

Despite the weather, Harrison dispatched a carriole, or small
sleigh, carrying Dr. Samuel McKeehan, Surgeon's Mate with
the Ohio Militia, Mr. Lemont, also of the Ohio Militia, and
Mr. Dubois, a French Canadian civilian, to the River Raisin.
McKeehan was to determine the situation of the wounded survivors of the Frenchtown action and provide them with any
medical assistance that he could render. Traveling under a flag
of truce, McKeehan was given one hundred dollars in gold,
a written copy of his orders, a letter of introduction that he
was to surrender to the first British officer that he might en-
counter, and an open letter to General Winchester.[6]

On the 31st, the temperature fell, changing rain to snow and
freezing solid the mud obstructing the roads. With the awaited
opportunity to advance now at hand, Harrison ordered that
the troops prepare to march at 6 o'clock the following morning. Leaving the Portage early on the morning of February 1,
they reached the Maumee Rapids early the following day.
Though the change in the weather had made Harrison's move-

ment to the Maumee possible, the enterprise was by no means
an easy one. Charged with the responsibility of transporting
eleven pieces of artillery, only one of which was mounted on
a wheeled carriage, the rest on sleds, Daniel Cushing of the
Second Regiment of Artillery wrote in his diary:

> Rose early and mustered all hands, the wagons froze
> into the mud very much, cut them loose with axes,
> pried them out of the mud, ate breakfast and mov-
> ed on, but with great difficulty, wagons sticking in
> the mud, sleds getting fast in the stumps.[7]

Nonetheless, the army had continued to advance. As the column moved onward, it passed through a field of standing Indian corn where a substantial number of ears still remained
upon the stalks. To the troops who had suffered through the
preceding days at the Portage on much reduced rations, the
tacit invitation provided by the abundant discovery proved too
great of a temptation to resist. A member of the Petersburg
Volunteers remembered that:

> As soon as we entered the inviting field the army
> broke in every direction, like a drove of frightened
> cattle. Deaf to the commands of our officers, and
> regardless of all military order, we tore down the
> precious ears, and filled our pockets and our
> bosoms till we were richly laden with the spoils of
> the field. With musket in one hand, and an ear of
> corn in the other, we marched on, greedily devour-
> ing the unstinted supply of a merciful Providence.
> No pound cake ever tasted half so delicious . . . We
> were amazed that we had lived so long in the world
> and had never discovered before the transcendent
> luxury of raw corn.[8]

Arriving at the Maumee, Harrison proceeded to a high bluff
on the south bank overlooking the foot of the river rapids. Here
he ordered that the site be cleared, a stockade erected, and that
the fortification be named Fort Meigs, in honor of Return
Jonathon Meigs, the Governor of Ohio. Harrison's choice of
location was a judicious one. The foot of the Rapids was the

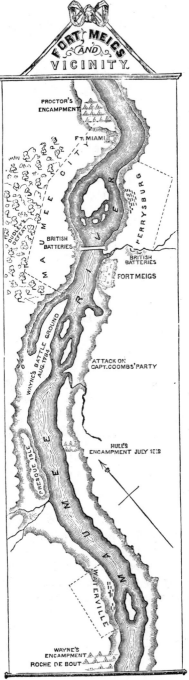

Fort Meigs & Vicinity

western terminus for men, equipment, and provisions moving westward by ship across Lake Erie and up the Maumee. Once at the Rapids, cargo being carried by vessels that could easily navigate the river to this point was required to be unloaded and transported overland to its destination, owing to the shallow depth of the water.

The shallowness of the Maumee along the Rapids also rendered this area the traditional land route of invasion into the Northwest both northward into Canada and southward into the United States. By effectively commanding the Rapids, Harrison could monitor and dictate the flow of supplies and provisions being sent westward into the interior across the Great Lakes, defend the Northwest from British attack, and control the corridor through which he planned to execute his invasion of Canada.

Although the north bank of the river afforded Harrison the higher ground, the commanding General remained on the south side to better secure his lines of provision and reinforcement. To compensate for the disadvantage in topography, the artillery batteries of the fort were to be elevated, or placed on high mounds of earth.

Harrison assigned the task of designing and supervising construction of the works to Captain Charles Gratiot of the US Corps of Engineers. Gratiot, an 1806 graduate of West Point, was the Northwest Army's chief engineer and was to serve Harrison with distinction throughout the course of the 1813 - 1814 campaigns. Indisposed at the time with a lingering illness, Gratiot only surveyed the site, delegating responsibility of overseeing the building of Fort Meigs to Captain Eleazor D. Wood. A classmate of Gratiot's at West Point, Wood, also of the Engineers, assumed control and proceeded with vigor.

The fort was to be constructed in the shape of an irregular ellipse, roughly 2,500 yards in circumference, the perimeter stockaded with logs fifteen feet in length and set three feet in the ground. Eight blockhouses of double timber and four elevated batteries were erected, as were powder magazines and storehouses. Timber and brush cleared from the site and not used as building material were transformed into abitis, an entanglement of stakes and limbs used in much the same manner as modern barbed-wire. The abitis was then placed in front of the vulnerable openings in the stockade caused by the placement of the artillery batteries.

Captain Wood, writing in his journal, recorded that the building of the fort:

> together with the ordinary fatigues of the camp, was an undertaking of no small magnitude. Besides, an immense deal of labor was to be performed in excavating ditches, making abitis, and clearing away the wood about the camp and all this to be done, too, at a time when the weather was extremely severe, and the ground so hard frozen that it was almost impossible to open it with a spade and pick-axe. But in the use of the axe, mattock and spade, consisted all the military knowledge of the army. So we fell to work to bury ourselves, and heard nothing of the enemy.[9]

After the site was selected and construction commenced, scouting parties were sent out to reconnoiter the area. In an abandoned house across the river, one party discovered a badly mutilated body, shot, tomahawked, and scalped. At the door of the cabin stood a carriole, on the rooftop, a white flag. Informed of the find, Harrison ordered that the body be returned to camp where it was identified as that of Mr. Lemont, one of the envoys that Harrison had sent from the Portage to the River Raisin.[10]

According to some Frenchmen who had joined with Harrison, the three men had come as far as the house the first evening after leaving Harrison. Stopping there to sleep for the night, they had placed the sleigh with the white flag flying at the front door, feeling secure in the protection that it offered. Their presence was discovered by a Captain William Elliot, a British officer stationed at Fort Malden who was leading a raiding party of about fifteen Indians.

Elliot, stated the Frenchmen, realized that the Indians would have no part in attacking a group protected by a flag of truce. He, therefore, sent a single Wyandot to the sleigh to remove the flag. This accomplished, the rest of the scouting party was sent forward to ambush the sleeping Americans. Creeping towards the cabin, the Indians fired their weapons, killing Lemont and wounding the others. After stripping and robbing the survivors, they and their horses were brought to Elliot who conducted his prisoners to Malden. Before leaving the scene, the Captain sent the Wyandot back to the house, where he tossed the white flag on the roof.

Elliot, it was claimed, had boasted of his ingenuity in deceiving the Indians into attacking, after returning to Amherstburg where he turned the Americans over to General Proctor.[11] Proctor immediately began to verbally abuse Dr. McKeehan. Though McKeehan was able to defend himself and his mission and was eventually permitted to tend to the wounded, Proctor ordered him arrested on March 2, and he was sent to a dungeon in Montreal where he remained imprisoned for thirty days.[12]

As the work on Fort Meigs progressed, Harrison continued to amass the troops of the Northwest in preparation for the invasion of Canada. Shortly after February 2, Harrison was joined by a regiment of Kentucky Volunteers and General Edward Tupper's Brigade of Ohio Militia, increasing his strength to over 2,000 men. Harrison then ordered that all of the troops of the left wing, except for one company at each of the six smaller forts in the area, be marched to the Rapids, giving him an aggregate command of nearly 3,300 effectives.

Harrison now was forced to proceed quickly if he was to accomplish the planned attack. Much of the force at his disposal consisted of militia whose six month term of enlistment was nearly expired. Harrison planned to postpone his invasion until just prior to the time the militia's tour of service would end. By waiting, Harrison hoped to accumulate as many troops as possible before launching the attack into Canada. Once the thrust had begun, Harrison expected that the innate patriotism of the militia would compel them to continue, even though their enlistment was over. Wrote Harrison to Secretary of War John Armstrong, "I had established with them (the militia) the principle that I had the right to march them to any point before the day which would complete their Six Month tour, and I knew them too well to believe that they would abandon me in the country of the enemy."[13]

On Monday the 8th, a company of spies who had been sent out to scout the area returned to camp with information that a war party of about 200 Indians was in the vicinity and that they had driven the cattle from a French settlement some fourteen miles from the fort. This information, verified by some French refugees who had sought shelter at the garrison, was relayed to Harrison who, faced with the shrinking terms of enlistment of his men and increasingly deteriorating weather conditions, had to act decisively if he was to salvage his winter campaign into Canada.[14]

Assembling a force of 600 men made up from all the brigades at his disposal, and another group of 500 to act as reserve, Harrison ordered the detachment to march from the fort with one day's provisions after the beating of the evening retreat, descend the river and engage the enemy. With Harrison and his staff leading the way and accompanied by a single six pound cannon, the 600 man force set out shortly after dark, followed an hour later by the reserves.

Traveling quickly downriver some 18 or 20 miles, Harrison discovered the abandoned campsite of the Indians. Waiting until his relief column had joined the main body, he ordered that the combined 1,100 man force proceed to the River Raisin. Marching on the frozen river two miles further, several of the mounted officers and their horses broke through the ice. Shortly thereafter the six pounder broke through as well, carrying its team into five feet of water. Leaving the gun crew and a company of Ohio Militia to extricate the piece, the army proceeded to a small island east of the mouth of the Maumee where they encamped for the night. As the contigent retired for the evening, spies were sent on to the Raisin to gather intelligence. Returning to the island early the next morning with a prisoner, the scouts reported that the Indians had been to Frenchtown, but had left the Raisin for Malden, taking the cattle with them.[15]

With the Indian party safely into undisputed British territory, his provisions insufficient to permit him to continue to the Raisin and make a stand, the terms of enlistment for his troops virtually expired, and the weather once again steadily deteriorating, Harrison was forced to return empty handed. Reversing the line of march, the army marched up the left side of the Bay, stopping briefly at the abandoned homes of some inhabitants who had fled in the face of increasing hostilities. Pausing only long enough to retrieve some corn which had been left in the houses, the army quickly completed their journey back to the fort.[16]

As Harrison returned and the troops of the expedition straggled back to camp, the commanding general abandoned all hope of completing his planned invasion. Writing the Secretary of War, Harrison explained:

> I have awaited with an anxiety which I cannot describe for a change in the weather, and until this day I never abandoned the hope of being able to execute the plan which I had formed. It is now, however, the 11th of the month. The period for which the Kentucky troops (which first took the field) were to serve expires in four days, as does that of four-fifths of Tupper's Brigade. These poor fellows have suffered so much that they have resisted the strong appeal to their patriotism backed by a most liberal offer of pay which has been made by their respective States. They will not engage for two or even one month, but if I were ready to advance, I am satisfied they would not hesitate to follow me. To persevere longer under the expectation of accomplishing the objects of the Campaign during the winter is, in my opinion, no longer proper, considering the enormous expense which a continuance of these efforts at this season daily produces and which would only be justified by a reasonable hope of success. Under present appearances, I can no longer indulge such hopes of success. Indeed, I fear that I shall be censured for having cherished them too long, and that I have sacrificed the public interest in a vain pursuit.[17]

On the 13th of February then, and during the weeks that followed, many of the militia regiments from Ohio and Kentucky were honorably discharged, leaving the fort protected by a competent, though much weakened force of Virginia and Pennsylvania Militia.[18] In addition, all the teams that had been hired for public service were discharged and the public oxen in the encampment were sent to settlements in the interior where forage was more readily and inexpensively available.[19]

In order to adequately garrison his position at the Rapids, Harrison now ordered that a recently activated battalion of

Ohio Militia and a company of regulars stationed at Fort Winchester at Defiance be brought forward to man the outposts along the Auglaize and St. Mary's rivers. Leaving only a Subaltern's command, approximately fifty men, at each of the posts along Hull's Trace and a company at both Upper and Lower Sandusky, the remaining troops, amounting to 1,500 - 1,800 men, were advanced to Fort Meigs. In addition, Harrison requested that Governor Shelby of Kentucky hold in readiness, but not call out, an additional 1,500 men.[20]

The site of the Rapids encampment became the scene of ever increasing activity. Stockading, earthworks, batteries, and blockhouses moved towards completion; supplies, provisions, ordnance and ammunition arrived daily. Troops whose enlistments had ended were paraded, discharged, and filed from the camp to be met by their incoming replacements.

Early on the morning of the 16th, sentinels hailed two strangers who appeared to be taking an uncommon interest in the progress of the fort. As the strangers approached the guard's fire and began to warm themselves, they asked many questions as to the garrison's strength and the number of cannons that were mounted. Their curiosity aroused the suspicion of the officer of the day, and they were apprehended and conducted to General Harrison. In Harrison's presence the men claimed to be civilians from the River Raisin area, and knowing that the fort was in short supply of flour, advised the General to send a small detachment to Frenchtown where they claimed that a large quantity of this provision was available. Harrison knew, however, that the Raisin had only recently been reinforced by a 600 man British detachment. Realizing that the men were spies, he ordered them arrested.[21]

The discovery of the British agents brought a sense of urgency to the encampment. Harrison assembled the garrison and announced that he felt an attack could occur at any time. Three 18 pound cannons were mounted on batteries, a 12 pounder was placed in readiness in the lower blockhouse, and the other twelves and sixes were supplied with powder and ball. Though the attack anticipated by Harrison failed to materialize, by the end of the week four 18 pounders, four iron twelves, one brass twelve, four sixes and five howitzers were mounted and battle-ready.[22]

With progress on the works proceeding in a satisfactory manner and the troop strength of the garrison increasing, Harrison devised a new, bold plan to take a limited offensive action against the enemy. The **Queen Charlotte**, a British vessel of seventeen guns and 400 tons, was presently moored fast in the ice less than 100 yards from Fort Malden. Harrison's scheme was to take a handpicked, volunteer force of about 100 men across the ice of Lake Erie to Amherstburg, board the ship under the cover of darkness, and ignite the vessel with incendiary explosives. Though not announcing his plan to the garrison, Harrison sought the discreet council of his senior officers, finally selecting Captain Angus L. Langham of the 19th Regiment of Infantry to lead the expedition. Major Amos Stoddard of the 1st Regiment of Artillery and Captain Wood were ordered to prepare the explosives.

On the 26th, an elite group of soldiers from the various commands of the fort were paraded and addressed by the General. Harrison, though not revealing the details of the mission, clearly stated the dangers involved and the fact that the enterprise would require the most rigid discipline and strictest silence. After the expedition was underway, he explained, the men would be informed of their mission; and then, at that time, if any felt that the object was too hazardous, they would be permitted to return to camp.

Marching immediately by way of Lower Sandusky, the force consisted of 68 regulars, 120 Pennsylvania and Virginia Militia, and 24 Indians, accompanied by 24 sleds and several pilots. Problems, however, immediately became apparent. Some of the Indians, imbibing freely of their whiskey rations, became intoxicated and quarrelsome. A black servant of Lieutenant Joseph Larwill by the name of Lewis exchanged words with a private in Lieutenant Maddis' company, and as the argument accelerated, Lewis was struck twice in the head with a tomahawk by the soldier, wounding him severely. Other members of the party became drunk and unruly as well.

On the 2nd of March shortly after 10:00, Langham called a halt, assembled his command, and described the mission in detail. Calling attention to the hazards of the journey to come, Langham again stressed that those thinking that the plan was too dangerous would be permitted to return. About fourteen men elected to stay at the present encampment, and six soldiers and an equal number of Indians returned to the Rapids. Taking to the march once more, the force proceeded quickly to Sandusky Bay where they set out across the ice. Almost at once one of the sleds broke through into shallow water. An Indian discovered on the perimeter of the detachment was captured and nearly executed before he was identified as belonging to the expedition, and as the party advanced across the lake, the alarm was sounded as an unidentified column appeared to approach from the north. A scouting party sent to reconnoiter returned and reported that the "column" was only a mirage caused by the sun reflecting on the frozen water.

The detachment paused for the evening on a small island. After supper they retired for the night, only to be awakened a short time later by the report of a guard's musket. Quickly the expedition took to their posts, ready for action. To the detachment's embarrassment, it was discovered that the guard had discharged his gun accidentally. Langham was furious over this serious breach of security. Ordering that the sentry be brought to him, the Captain recommended that he be summarily shot for his indescretion. Cooler heads prevailed, however, and as this was the soldier's first offense, the incident was allowed to go unpunished after the guard pledged on his honor that his actions had been unintentional. On account of the alarm, though, security for the camp was increased and two parties of Indians were sent out to patrol above and below the encampment. The night passed without further incident.

The following morning the detachment advanced to South Bass Island near Put-in-Bay. A scouting party reported that the ice had broken up and the lake was open less than a quarter mile from the island's shore. Langham conferred with the guides who reported that the mission now seemed impossible to execute.

The broken ice here, claimed the guides, indicated that the Detroit River was also open, as was the water from Middle Sister Island to the mainland. While it might be possible to traverse the lake as far north as Middle Sister, the remainder of the route would be most difficult, and to ascend the Detroit after dark, fire the **Charlotte**, and safely retreat would be nearly impossible. In addition, should the weather worsen, or if the wind should shift to the south, the guides predicted that the entire detachment would be left stranded and highly vulnerable.

Langham was under orders not to proceed if the guides

thought it unsafe. Though in agreement with his pilots, Langham decided to consult with his officers before making a decision. A hastily called council likewise agreed unanimously that to proceed would be ill-advised. That night the weather once again turned cold, reviving a faint hope that the expedition might yet continue. At the break of day the following morning, another council was held; and although the weather seemed to be cooperating at least temporarily, it was again the opinion of the officers that the advantages tendered by the present circumstances were too tenuous to warrant continuing, leaving the Captain with no choice but to abandon the mission.

Langham called his men together and informed them of the decision. Calling their attention to the importance that the government had attached to the success of the mission, Langham softened the embarrassment of retreat by reminding the men that this contingent represented the prime of the army, and their loss in a mission with no chance of success would place an unconscionable burden on the security of the Northwest. Langman then asked the men their opinion on whether or not to proceed, and although a few zealots voted to continue, the majority surrendered to the judgment of the guides and officers.

Accordingly, the detachment began the return. Moving on a westwardly course, the force was met by a messenger from Harrison, stating that the General was most concerned for the safety of the expedition. Through his envoy, Harrison again reiterated his orders that if in the opinion of the officers or guides the safety of the troops during the mission or retreat was seriously compromised by the weather, then the endeavor was not to be attempted. Should the mission be abandoned, ordered Harrison, the force was to proceed immediately to Presque Isle in the upper end of the Maumee Bay. Harrison's timely dispatch did much to counter the disappointment of the men as they set off towards the mouth of the Maumee River.[23]

Arriving at Presque Isle on the morning of March 5, the detachment was met by Harrison and a detail from the fort to escort them back to the camp. Harrison, with his third attempt to take action against the British in as many months producing no results, now turned his full attention to completing the fortification at the Rapids, hoping to accumulate the men and provisions necessary to take more productive action the

William Henry Harrison

Lossing, Ohio Historical Society

Tecumseh

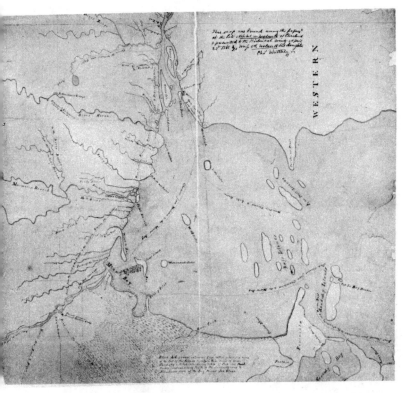

Western Basin of Lake Erie
*Map of the Western Basin of Lake Erie drawn c.
1813 by Ashbel Walworth. Note the location of Fort
Meigs, Frenchtown, Detroit, and Fort Malden.*

Fort Malden National Historic Site

A View of Amherstburg, c. 1813.

following spring.

Harrison knew his position on the Maumee was secure for the moment. Although the continuing problem of expiring enlistments was once more eroding the troop strength of the garrison, Harrison could again replenish his ranks by drawing on newly organized units from Ohio and Kentucky. Therefore, Governor Meigs, at Harrison's request, ordered that two brigades be activated and rendezvous in Dayton. The response to Meigs' call, however, was far less than adequate to reinforce the fort.[24] Governor Shelby of Kentucky likewise ordered 3,000 militia of that state to be drafted and organized under the command of Brigadier General Green Clay.[25]

The uncooperative weather which had checked Harrison's every attempt to strike against the British now was working to his advantage. With Lake Erie still frozen, Harrison reasoned that a concerted attack by the British against the Rapids would have to be postponed until the spring thaw opened the lake to navigation, probably no sooner than the first of April. This delay afforded Harrison the opportunity to return to Cincinnati to visit his ailing family, and to stop frequently as he crossed the state to lobby for and recruit the additional troops needed to bring the fort to a position of readiness.[26]

On Saturday, March 6, Harrison departed Fort Meigs for the Ohio River. Before leaving, Harrison assigned Captain Wood, who had been supervising the construction of the fortification, to leave the Rapids and travel to Lower Sandusky (present day Fremont, Ohio) to assist in the erecting of Fort Stephenson. In Wood's absence, the responsibility of completing Fort Meigs was delegated to General Leftwich.

Harrison was correct in assuming that the British were awaiting the opening of Lake Erie to launch a major offensive against Fort Meigs. Nonetheless, the fort had become the focus of an ever increasing tempo of vigilance and harassment from small parties of marauding Indian warriors and British spies. A work detail, sent away from the fort, was approached by two men, one of whom wore a uniform hidden under his coat. Pausing to chat with the fatigue party, one of the strangers asked:

"How many men do you suppose we have in camp, I suppose 1,000 strong." Our men, suspecting by this time that they might be enemies come to find out our strength and situation of our encampment, answered him "Yes, we are upwards of 3,000 strong." He then asked whether we did not expect a reinforcement, and how many. Our man answered that 4,000 were on the way and near at hand. One of the (strangers) parted from the other. Suspecting that . . . a party of Indians might be laid in ambush, our men then made the earliest opportunity to escape, they being unarmed.[27]

Another unarmed work party, sent to Fort Miami on the opposite side of the river to collect grass for bedding, was ambushed by Indians. Giving the alarm, the soldiers escaped by swimming the ice swollen Maumee and running back to the garrison. When first fired upon, one of the detail, a lieutenant, fell dead, and a second soldier was struck but without injury, the enemy's ball lodging in a Psalm Book carried in his tail pocket.[28] Late in the evening of March 9, Lieutenant William Walker of the Pennsylvania Line, who had left the fort to hunt ducks was reported missing. Early the next morning his tomahawked and scalped body was discovered some three miles below the fort, stuffed under the ice.[29]

As pressure from the enemy increased outside the stockade walls, the living conditions within steadily declined. The spring thaw, intermittent rains, and the activity of the men about the garrison had turned the marshy grounds into a virtual swamp, and the reserves of firewood and forage became critically depleted. Wrote Captain Cushing:

> Our camp is overwhelmed with mud and water, my eyes never saw such a place for mankind to live in, not a marquee or tent in the whole encampment but what has more or less mud and water in it, and what makes it much worse is for the want of wood. The timber is all cut off for a long distance from camp and there are no teams to haul any for the men, not a bushel of forage in this place, what teams we have cannot work, for they have nothing to eat. Our men are very sickly, no wonder, two or three die everyday, and I expect the deaths to increase . . .[30]

On March 17, Saint Patrick's Day, the men in camp made their grievances known. During the night a paddy, or dummy, stuffed with straw and "tolerably well dressed" was surreptitiously fashioned and placed on the chimney of Mr. Wheaton, the camp quartermaster. In his hand was placed a placard with the legend "The devil has come from Britain to see old Captain Wheaton" at the top, and a narrative of the camp inadequacies below:[31]

> It is observed by all the officers, some of them (in service) in the Revolutionary War, that this is the most disagreeable encampment they ever saw. It is impossible to pass from one tent to another without being over shoe mouth in mud, much less the streets of the encampment where it is ½ leg deep. Some (of the troops) indeed have puncheons to lay on which affords them some little relief from the damp, (but) you cannot go into any tent in camp without feeling for the sufferings of the occupants. You then begin to lose sight of your own situation, seeing many worse than your own. Scarcely any of the troops have more than one blanket to lay on, which is too little at the inclement season of the year and situation of our encampment.[32]

For the present the grumblings of the men went unanswered.

Though the increasing enemy activity around the fort underscored the necessity of completing the fortification as quickly as possible, progress on the works faltered and finally stopped completely under the direction of General Leftwich. Leftwich, an officer of far less ability than Harrison and lacking the technical expertise of Captain Wood, failed to assert his authority at the garrison. Instructed to "prosecute the lines of defense with all possible vigor," Leftwich's orders were ignored repeatedly by the militia under his command with impunity. Though the militia's refusal to follow orders caused the work to grind to a virtual standstill, endangering the lives of the entire encampment, Leftwich permitted his troops to stay in their quarters all day, justifying his decision by saying that since he "couldn't make the militia do anything, they might as well be in their tents as to be kept out of the mud and water.''

Indeed, once allowed to neglect their duty, the very troops assigned to build the fort proceeded to appropriate the timber brought into camp for use in constructing picketting and blockhouses and burn it for firewood. And as this convenient source of fuel was exhausted, the men were permitted to tear down sections of the stockade wall that had already been constructed and burn them as well. Captains Croghan, Bradford and Langham bitterly complained to Leftwich about the conduct of his men, but the General refused to take action.

When Wood returned from Fort Stephenson about the 20th of March, he was justifiably horrified at the negligent conduct of the "phlegmatic, stupid old granny." Personally reassuming the command of the project, Wood "found great difficulty in stopping the militia from destroying his works, but much greater in getting them to repair the breaches and depredations already committed on the lines."[33]

The reports from civilians and prisoners brought to the fort indicating that the British were close to launching their attack against the Rapids were increasing. Harrison, therefore, began his return to the fort, stopping first at Newport, Kentucky to meet with three companies of reinforcements raised in that state. Furnishing a pack horse to every two men, Harrison ordered them to proceed to the Rapids as quickly as possible. By courier, Harrison sent two dispatches to the fort. One relieved Leftwich of command and assigned his duties to Amos Stoddard. The second was an appeal to the members of the Virginia and Pennsylvania Militias whose period of enlistment was about to expire near the first of April. Reinforcements for the garrison were presently on their way to the fort. The inclemency of the weather, however, had delayed their march, and it was predicted that they would not arrive at the Rapids before the 10th or 15th of April. Harrison requested that the militia voluntarily extend their enlistments until the relief column arrived, guaranteeing the safety of the encampment.

To the Virginians, the appeal fell on deaf ears, and on the 2nd and 4th of the month they departed from camp with General Leftwich leading the way. The Pennsylvania soldiers, however, were addressed by Brigadier General Richard Crooks who appealed to their patriotism, solicited their continuing service, and offered an additional twelve dollars a month to those who chose to remain. Asking his men to give his proposal careful deliberation, he ordered that his command assemble at 7 a.m. the next day and return their decision. The following morning, as the Pennsylvania troops were paraded:

> The General gave orders that all those who desired to volunteer their services at the word "Shoulder Arms, Foward" will shoulder and advance four paces in front of the line. At the word "Shoulder Arms" our company shouldered and marched unanimously, the whole amount of volunteers was 205.[34]

As the reports of an impending attack increased and the troop strength of the post again ebbed, security for the fort was intensified and discipline within the camp rigidly enforced. Near the end of March, John T. Mosby, a private in Captain Bradford's Company of Infantry, let it be known that he intended to desert to the British, but not before he had exploded the post's powder magazine. Apprehended before he could put his plot into action and brought before a court martial, Mosby was tried and pronounced guilty. His sentence:

> To be confined, tied to a post or log in a tent by himself one month, to have a handcuff on his right hand, to ride a wooden horse 30 minutes once a week for a month with a six pound ball fastened to each foot, to wear a ball and chain the whole time, to have one eyebrow and one side of his head shaved, and to be fed on bread and water only. After the time of confinement expires, he is to be drummed out of camp.[35]

The completion of the fort and the ordinary fatigues of the camp were the activities taking most of the time of the men in garrison. Though the work was arduous and routine, it was not all consuming, and the spare moments afforded the troops were filled with leisure and reflection. A soldier from the Independent Volunteer Battalion corresponding with a friend in Virginia, wrote that "We visit each other's tents . . . sing, tell stories, play music, and drink grog when we can get it, which bye-the-bye, is not often, suttlers not being permitted to sell spirits in the camp.''[36] Sergeant Keen noted that:

> Great quantities of fish are caught. Of (the) different sorts, perch from 3 to 10 pounds, muskellunge from 3 to 40 pound weight, sturgeon from 1 to 100 weight, cat 100. These fish are taken with a spear, the handle to be 12 feet in length . . . About the break of day myself and one more went to the river to spear some fish. In the space of thirty minutes we had 67 fish which weighed from 1 to 7 pounds. We caught them all by walking up the shore and plunging our spears in by random. Caught sometimes 3 and frequently 2 at a stroke.[37]

As Sergeant Keen harvested the natural bounty of the Maumee, Captain Cushing delighted in its beauty:

> At this time, this is the most romantic looking place that ever my eyes saw; to look from the battery on to the river and meadows is the greatest charm of any place that ever was in any country that ever I traveled in; the water is gliding through the meadows swiftly and covered with all kinds of water fowl, and the ice which was left by the high water on the meadows is without bounds from three to fifteen feet deep, and that over more than half of the bottoms.[38]

On the 8th of April, a seven man work detail under the command of Sergeant John Kelly of the Artillery left the stockade and traveled to a wooded area some 400 yards up river from the fort to gather timber. The men, some of them leaving their muskets stacked against a nearby tree, went about their business unaware that they had been discovered by a band of fifteen Indians. The raiding party silently crept toward the unsuspecting Americans, waiting until they had come between the men and their horses before launching the attack. Felix Rudes, who had been driving the teams, fell dead; Kelly and Joseph Patterson were taken prisoners.

At once three detachments were dispatched from the fort to pursue the Indians and their captives, one sent up river by land, and two sent downstream by boat in hopes of intercepting the prisoners. The force traveling on the shore quickly became separated from one another and returned to the garrison unable to render any assistance. Of the two parties in boats, one, commanded by Lieutenant David Gwyinn, pursued the Indians for about five miles, but gave up the chase and also returned.

The second boat, manned by twelve French civilians, came upon the Indians about a half mile below where Gwyinn had turned back. As the Frenchmen approached, the Indians dispersed, five taking to land and ten remaining in the water in two canoes. As the forces converged, a brisk fire broke out from both sides. Five Indians were shot dead and three wounded. Of the Frenchmen, seven were wounded, two mortally. The prisoners, however, were not recaptured as the surviving Indians made good their escape. The following morning, a relief column led by Captain Langham discovered the hastily abandoned campsite of the Indians. There, with some horses and equipment, Langham found two canoes, blood stained and riddled with bullet holes. Kelly and Patterson, though, had disappeared with their captors.[39]

Harrison returned to the Rapids on April 12,[40] and was greeted with a salute by fifteen of the fort's cannons. Congratulating Stoddard and the men of the garrison for their good conduct during his absence, the commanding General now urged that every man devote "all his thoughts and all his strength" to the completion of the nearly finished fortification. The expected attack of the British was at hand, claimed Harrison, and he promised that any soldier who distinguished himself, either in combat or in readying the fort's defenses, would be recommended to the President and the Governor of his state.[41]

On the 18th, a party of spies returned from the River Raisin, bringing with them three Frenchmen who "rejoiced at the opportunity of escape." The three claimed that in Frenchtown there were many others like them, wishing to join the Americans, but hesitant because of the increasing number of hostile Indians and British in the area. The Frenchmen also reported that the British expedition against Fort Meigs was underway, and that the garrison could expect the attack within ten to twelve days. Even now, they related, Tecumseh was at Detroit threatening all those who refused to come with him and attack the fort with death and the destruction of their property.[42]

Fort Meigs stood virtually completed. Enclosing nearly ten acres, and encircled with stockading, ditches and abitis, the fortification contained two earthen powder magazines, a quartermaster's building and various other storehouses and work areas. At each gate a guard tower and gallery was erected, and spaced along the stockade were five artillery batteries displaying an impressive array of 18, 12 and 6 pound cannons and howitzers. Projecting at an angle from the perimeter wall were seven two-story blockhouses, each containing an artillery piece and its crew on the lower floor, and manned on the upper story with a detachment of rifle and musket men. An eighth blockhouse, nearly completed, in the southeast corner of the fort, was ordered partially torn down and converted into a high, elevated battery. Below the garrison on the broad flood plain were placed the articifer yards, and projecting into the Maumee River was a boat dock, forming a loading and repair facility for shallow draught river vessels.

Within the camp a vast sea of tents housed 1,100 effectives, well supplied and provisioned. The officers of the garrison were assigned to command designated areas of the fort. Each soldier was issued ten rounds of buckshot cartridges and received explicit instructions as to his response in case of an attack, whether it be manning the stockade wall or waiting in reserve within the fort's interior. Additional ammunition was dispersed and ready for distribution to the troops should the need arise. To attack and reduce the fortification would be a formidable challenge. In the opinion of Captain Wood, Fort Meigs was well prepared for the test of British artillery.[43]

Strict attention was paid to the security of the camp, and the drilling of the troops intensified. Guards mounting the watch towers were ordered to call out "All's well," starting at the main gate and continuing around the encampment every fifteen minutes. Fatigue parties leaving the stockade were given extra protection, and details sent to the river to fish were required to take their weapons. At the rotation of the guards the discharged sentinels were permitted to fire their muskets at a target, the best shot receiving an extra quart of whiskey, and the second best a pint. The firing of two guns or a cannon was to be used as a signal to call the entire camp to alarm, at which time all in the garrison were to move to their battle stations.[44]

The long predicted engagement with the British was at hand. On the 29th of April, Harrison addressed his command:

> It is at length reduced to certainty that the enemy are about to carry into effect their threatened attack upon this post. The temerity of the attempt can only be accounted for by their ignorance of our strength or their reliance upon our want of resolution to defend ourselves. The General is confident that in both they will be woefully disappointed. Can the citizens of a free country who have taken up arms to defend its rights think of submitting to a band composed of the mercenaries of reluctant Canadians goaded to the field by the bayonet and wretched naked savages? Can the breast of an American soldier when he casts his eyes to the opposite shore, the scene of his country's triumphs over the same foes be influenced by any other feeling than the hopes of victory and glory, is not this army composed of the same materials which fought and conquered under the immortal Wayne? Yes fellow soldiers, your General sees your countenances beam with the same fire that he witnessed upon that glorious occasion. And although it would be the height of presumption to compare himself to a Hero, he boasts of being that Hero's pupil. To your posts, then fellow soldiers, and remember that the eyes of your country are upon you.[45]

Notes for Chapter II

[1] Robert B. McAfee, **History of the Late War in the Western Country,** (Bowling Green: Historical Publications Company, 1919), pp. 257-58; Richard C. Knopf, ed., **Document Transcriptions of The War of 1812 In The Northwest,** Vol. 7, pt. 1, **Letters To The Secretary of War 1813 Relating To The War of 1812 In The Northwest,** (Columbus: Ohio Historical Society, 1961), "McClenahan to Harrison, January 26, 1813," pp. 61-62; Richard C. Knopf, ed., **Document Transcriptions of The War of 1812 In The Northwest,** Vol. 1, **William Henry Harrison and The War of 1812,** (Columbus: Ohio Historical Society, 1956), "Harrison to _____, January 24, 1813," pp. 77-79.

[2] Richard C. Knopf, ed., **Document Transcriptions of The War of 1812 In The Northwest,** Vol. 2, pt. 2, **The National Intelligencer Reports The War of 1812 In The Northwest,** (Columbus: Ohio Historical Society, 1958), "Horrid Disaster," & Wm. H. Harrison to His Exc. Gov. Meigs, January 24, 1813," pp. 18-19.

[3] McAfee, **History of the Late War,** p. 258.

[4] Sally L. Young, ed., "To The Rapids, A Journal of a Tour of Duty in the Northwestern Army Under the Command of Major-General Wm. Henry Harrison, by Sergeant Greenbury Keen, First Regiment, Second Brigade, Pennsylvania Militia," (Unpublished manuscript, Ohio Historical Society), pp. 18-19.

[5] Ibid., p. 19.

[6] Knopf, **Letters To The Secretary of War 1813,** pt. 1, "Harrison to Armstrong, February 11, 1813," pp. 96-99.

[7] Harlow Lindley, ed., **Fort Meigs and the War of 1812, Orderly Book of Cushing's Company, 2nd U. S. Artillery April, 1813 - February, 1814, and Personal Diary of Captain Daniel Cushing October, 1812 - July, 1813,** (Columbus: Ohio Historical Society, 1975), p. 97; also "Selections from the Gano Papers," **Quarterly Publication of The Historical and**

Philosophical Society of Ohio 16 (1921), "Alexander Meeks to General John S. Gano, January 21, 1813": 29-31.

[8] Alfred M. Lorrain, **The Helm, The Sword, And The Cross: A Life Narrative**, (Cincinnati: Poe & Hitchcock, 1862), pp. 120-21.

[9] Robert B. Boehm and Randall L. Buchman, eds., **Journal of The Northwestern Campaign of 1812 - 1813 Under Major-General Wm. H. Harrison by Bvt. Lieut.-Colonel Eleazer D. Wood, Captain Corps of Engineers, U. S. Army**, (Defiance: The Defiance College Press, 1975), p. 8.

[10] "The Gano Papers," "Alexander Meeks to General John Sites Gano, February 4, 1813," pp. 42-43.

[11] Joseph H. Larwill, "Journal of Joseph H. Larwill Relating to Occurences Transpired in the Service of the U States Commencing April 5, 1812," (Unpublished manuscript, Burton Historical Collection, Detroit Public Library), p.29.

[12] McAfee, **History of the Late War**, p. 260; Richard C. Knopf, ed., **Document Transcriptions of The War of 1812 in The Northwest**, Vol. 10, pt. 2, **Western Reserve Historical Society War of 1812 Collection**, (Columbus: Ohio Historical Society, 1962), "Ensign Church to His wife, Jerusha, February 11, 1813," p. 67; Knopf, **The National Intelligencer Reports**, pt. 2, "Affidavit of Medard Labbadie, February 11, 1813," pp. 31-32; "Dr. M'Keehan's Narrative, May 24, 1813," pp. 124-25; **Michigan Pioneer and Historical Collections in 40 Volumes**, Vol. 15, "Samuel M'Keehan to Lieut. Dudley, Montreal Prison, May 6, 1813," p. 280.

[13] Knopf, **Letters To The Secretary of War 1813**, pt. 1, "Harrison to Armstrong, February 11, 1813," p. 96.

[14] Lindley, **Fort Meigs**, p. 90.

[15] Larwill, "Journal," pp. 31-33.

[16] Ibid., p. 32; Knopf, **The National Intelligencer Reports**, pt. 2, "From **The Fredonian**, Extra, February 18, 1813," p. 31; Richard C. Knopf, ed., **Document Transcriptions of The War of 1812 In The Northwest**, Vol. 2, **Return Jonathon Meigs Jr. and The War of 1812**, (Columbus: Ohio Historical Society, 1957), "George Tod to Meigs, February 11, 1813," p. 73.

[17] Knopf, **Letters To The Secretary of War 1813**, pt. 1, "Harrison to Armstrong, February 11, 1813," pp. 96-99.

[18] Knopf, **Western Reserve Historical Society Collection**, pt. 2, "General Orders, Camp Meigs, February 23, 1813," p. 69; Charles S. Van Tassel, **Story of the Maumee Valley, Toledo, and the Sandusky Region**, (Chicago: S. G. Clarke Publishing Company, 1929), p. 577.

[19] Knopf, **Letters To The Secretary of War 1813**, pt. 1, "Harrison to Armstrong, February 11, 1813," pp. 96-99.

[20] Ibid.

[21] Young, "To the Rapids," p. 24.

[22] Lindley, **Fort Meigs**, p. 102.

[23] Larwill, "Journal," pp. 37-41; Knopf, **Letters To The Secretary of War 1813**, pt. 1, "Harrison to Armstrong, March 12, 1813," pp. 167-68.

[24] Knopf, **Western Reserve Historical Society Collection**, pt. 2, "R. J. Meigs to Major Genl. Wadsworth, March 21, 1813," p. 72.

[25] Knopf, **Letters To The Secretary of War 1813**, pt. 1, "Shelby to Armstrong, March 20, 1813," pp. 184-87.

[26] Knopf, **Western Reserve Historical Society Collection**, pt. 2, "Harrison to General T. H. Cushing, April 24, 1813," pp. 97-98.

[27] Larwill, "Journal," p. 44.

[28] Ibid., p. 43; Lindley, **Fort Meigs**, p. 104; Boehm and Buchman, **Wood's Journal**, p. 14.

[29] Lindley, **Fort Meigs**, p. 104; Larwill, "Journal," p. 43; Knopf, **The National Intelligencer Reports**, pt. 2, "April 5, 1813," p. 66; "Extract of a letter from an officer of rank in the Northwestern Army, to one of the editors dated March 9 (1813)," p. 74.

[30] Lindley, **Fort Meigs**, pp. 105-06; see also James Eubank, "The Seige of Fort Meigs," **Kentucky Historical Society Register** 19 (1921): 51.

[31] Lindley, **Fort Meigs**, p. 105.

[32] Larwill, "Journal," pp. 49-50.

[33] Boehm and Buchman, **Wood's Journal**, pp. 13-14.

[34] Young, "To The Rapids," p. 31; Knopf, **Letters To The Secretary of War 1813**, pt. 2, "Harrison to Armstrong, April 21, 1813," pp. 50-52.

[35] Lindley, **Fort Meigs**, p. 109.

[36] "Picture of a Soldier's Life, Letter from a Private in McRae's Company to a friend in Petersburg," **Niles Weekly Register**, March 28, 1813.

[37] Young, "To The Rapids," p. 30; **Niles Weekly Register**, July 17, 1813.

[38] Lindley, **Fort Meigs**, p. 106.

[39] Ibid., pp. 111-12; Knopf, **The National Intelligencer Reports**, pt. 2, "Private Correspondence, April 5, 1813," p. 40.

[40] Knopf, **Letters To The Secretary of War 1813**, pt. 2, "Harrison to Armstrong, April 5, 1813," p. 40.

[41] Lindley, **Fort Meigs**, p. 6.

[42] "Charles Marvin to Joseph H. Larwill, April 27, 1813," personal letter, (Larwill Family Papers, Archives-Library Collection, Ohio Historical Society); Knopf, **Letters To The Secretary of War 1813**, pt. 2, "Harrison to Armstrong, April 21, 1813," pp. 50-52.

[43] Boehm and Buchman, **Wood's Journal**, p. 7.

[44] Lindley, **Fort Meigs**, pp. 10-20.

[45] Ibid., p. 20.

Chapter 3

On April 24, Proctor had launched the attack against Fort Meigs after assembling troops and provisions at Malden for nearly a month. A respectable sized flotilla consisting of the Brig **Lady Prevost**, six other vessels of similar size, two gunboats, the **Eliza** and the **Myers**, and numerous bateaux, carried the British expedition from Fort Malden down the Detroit River and across Lake Erie towards the mouth of the Maumee River. With Proctor was a force of 522 regulars, most from the 41st Regiment of Foot, and 462 Canadian Militia, heavily strengthened with seige artillery and howitzers.[1] Traveling concurrently with the army, though over land, were a small detachment of Indian and Marine Department officials and a few volunteers from the Detroit and River Raisin areas.

On the 26th, an advance party of mounted British and Indian scouts appeared across the Maumee from Fort Meigs, where they spent a considerable time inspecting the American fortification and surveying the north bank for possible locations for their artillery batteries. Though their presence was immediately detected, the spies went unchallenged. The alarm sounded by the American sentries had thrown the fort into a state of confusion. An artillery crew manning one of the fort's 18 pound cannon was ordered to fire upon the visitors. Another crew responsible for transporting powder and ball to the piece did not receive the command to bring the ammunition forward, however, and although the British party stood in open view of the fort for about fifteen minutes, "exciting admiration and respect for their courage" among the men of the garrison, they had vanished unmolested before the ammunition was at long last distributed.[2]

On the 27th, Proctor's fleet entered the mouth of the Maumee and sailed to Swan Creek, about thirteen miles northwest of Fort Meigs. Here Proctor joined with Tecumseh, Roundhead, and approximately 1,000 Indian warriors, bringing the combined total of British soldiers, militia, and Indians to nearly 2,400. After holding a council with Tecumseh and his Chiefs and finalizing the plan of attack, Proctor once more pushed off for the Rapids, sending another mounted party ahead to scout the American position.[3]

This day the Americans were ready. As the British detachment approached the fort they discovered an American detail fishing at the river. Attacking the work party the British failed to inflict any casualties. As the Americans made their retreat to the safety of the fort, the artillery batteries along the stockade opened fire upon the attackers. The British responded with a volley of musket fire, and then retreated to a small ravine where they remained hidden for a short time. As they attempted to continue their retreat, another volley of cannon fire was sent them, possibly killing two.[4]

The following morning a small detachment under the command of Captain Hamilton of the Ohio Militia was sent upriver from the fort to determine the enemy's strength. Returning shortly after he had left, Hamilton reported that the British were from 1,500 to 2,000 strong and were at present unloading men, artillery and equipment below the ruins of old Fort Miami in preparation for the attack.[5]

Harrison quickly dispatched messengers from the fort with a warning of the British invasion to Upper and Lower Sandusky, and Governor Meigs in Franklinton. He also sent an urgent appeal, carried by Captain William Oliver, to General Green Clay and a 1,200 man relief force from Kentucky.[6] Clay, who was moving towards the Rapids from up the river over the same route taken by General Winchester, was ordered to advance to the fort as quicky as possible.[7]

It was obvious that the fort was to undergo an extended artillery siege. To protect his men from the enemy's guns, Harrison ordered that traverses, mounds of earth twenty feet thick at the base and twelve feet high, be constructed extending the length of the fort's interior. Dividing the entire garrison into three work parties, he instructed each party to work an eight hour shift, thus allowing work on the new defenses to proceed around the clock. To prevent the British from learning of the traverses being constructed within the post, Harrison ordered that the tents of the encampment be pitched on the British side of the new works, shielding the traverses' location and progress from the enemy.[8]

The British, too, spent the remainder of the day preparing for battle. Establishing their main camp at Fort Miami, artillery, including two 24 pound cannon captured from the Americans at Detroit,[9] and equipment was unloaded and moved upriver to within range of the American position. As the British and Canadian soldiers fell to work constructing their gun batteries, Tecumseh's Indians were sent across the river to invest the fort and annoy the defenders with musket fire.

Although the Americans were aware of the position of the British gun emplacements, Harrison had only 360 rounds of ammunition for the fort's 18 pound cannon, and he ordered that these guns be fired only sparingly, permitting the British to proceed with their construction for the most part unchallenged. Throughout the 28th, 29th, and 30th, both armies prepared their defenses. And although each side fired upon the other as the works were being completed, these exchanges were tentative and probing in character, inflicting few casualties. During the night of the 30th, the two British gunboats, the **Eliza** and the **Myers**, moved upstream to the foot of the Rapids under the cover of darkness and fired upon the fort, but with little effect.[10]

As dawn broke on May 1, the contestants on both sides of the Maumee were prepared for battle. When the British gunners across the river began to sight their weapons in on the American position, Harrison ordered that the tents of the garrison which had hidden the fort's traverses from the British be struck and moved to the protection of the encampment's interior. The moving of the tents,

was done in almost a moment, and that beautiful

prospect of beating up our quarters, which but an instant before presented itself to the view of the eager and skillful (British) artillerists, had now entirely fled, and in its place, suddenly appeared an immense shield of earth, obscuring from his sight every tent, every horse, (of which there were 200) and every creature belonging to the camp.[11]

Nonetheless, the British hoisted their standard and commenced the bombardment. Within Fort Meigs the troops took to their battle stations, and civilians who had been caught inside by the arrival of the British were pressed into service and ordered to do likewise.[12] Hurling shot and shell from 24, 12, and 6 pound cannon and eight inch mortars, the attackers fired 240 rounds into camp throughout the course of the day as the Indians harassed the Americans from the rear.[13]

As the attack continued, the defenders responded with a constant, though restrained, fire from the fort's artillery. To increase the limited supply of cannon balls, Harrison ordered that each British ball fired into the stockade, retrieved by an American, and turned in to the camp Quartermaster, would be redeemed for a gill, four ounces, of whiskey. Over the course of the battle over 1,000 gills were thus awarded the troops. During the bombardment:

> One of our militia men took his station on the embankment and gratuitously forewarned us of every shot. In this he became so skillful that he could, in almost every case, predict the destination of the ball. As soon as he saw the smoke issue from the muzzle of the gun, he would cry out "shot" or "bomb" as the case might be. "Look out, main battery," "Blockhouse number one," "Now for the meat house," "Good bye if you will pass." The brave fellow continued to maintain his post, despite the expostulations of his friends, until one shot came which defied all his calculations. Silent, motionless, perplexed, he stood for a moment, and then he was swept into eternity. In his zeal, the unfortunate hero forgot to consider that when there was no obliquity in the issue of the smoke, either

to the right or left, above or below, the fatal messenger was traveling in the direct line of his vision.[14].

On the 2nd, the British continued the attack. This day, in addition to shelling the entire garrison as they had previously, the enemy now began to throw forge heated, red hot cannon balls at the fort's powder magazines. Heated balls such as these, crashing through the magazine's roof would be capable of igniting all of the explosives stored within it, causing a blast of enough force to level the post. The fort's two magazines were stoutly built. The walls were below ground and constructed of double timber, and the roofs were of alternating layers of wood and leather hides, both mounded over with earth. Nonetheless, the constant fire from the British gunners slowly began to eat away at the structures' protection.

Colonel Alexander Bourne of the Ohio Militia, commanding a fatigue party ordered by Captain Wood to throw up an entrenchment near one of the magazines, noted that:

> The ground was much exposed, being nearly in range of the magazine, at which the enemy were throwing red hot balls to blow it up, and these balls passed between the men, and hissed and boiled in the bank. The men would leave their work, and declare they could not stand it. I informed Captain Wood that the men could not be kept at work. He then gave me an unlimited order on the Commissary for whiskey, and directed me to give it to them every half hour, and make them drink it until they were insensible to fear, but not too drunk to stand and work. He said "There is no other way, it must be done in extreme cases!" And so I did it; the men then kept at their work, reeling and cursing the British and their hot balls, until the work was finished. There were none killed or badly wounded.[15]

Slowly, the constant pressure of the British fire eroded the earthen protection of one of the camp's magazines, and a party of volunteers was sent to repair the damage.

While we were desperately at work, a bomb shell fell upon the roof, and lodging in one of the braces, commenced spinning. Instantly we fell prostrate on our faces, and, in breathless horror, awaited the tremendous explosion which was expected to end our earthly career. Only one of the party exercised his calm reason, and silently argued that, as the shell had not exploded as quickly as usual, something might be wrong in its arrangement. In any event, death was inevitable if it was not extinguished, and the brave fellow, springing to his feet, seized a boat hook, pulled the hissing bomb to the ground, and jerked the burning fuse from its socket.[16]

The magazine was repaired before further damage could occur.

The artillery exchange continued, vigorously executed by the British, answered with restraint by the Americans. As the day wore on:

The garrison frequently showed itself above the works, and occasionally gave three cheers, especially when the fire of the enemy was not as brisk, and when it could be done with safety. It always occasioned a most hideous **yell** from the Indians. These rascals appeared to be greatly delighted at the bursting of the shells in our camp, and whenever great or material damage was supposed to have been done by an explosion, they were sure to express their approbation by **yelping**.[17]

Another observer, however, noted that:

F. Sutton, Quartermaster of our regiment, was constitutionally a coward. He was so much afraid of being killed that he could not eat, and said that he did not sleep during the siege. He generally sat crouched down behind a pile of three or four hundred barrels of flour, and while several men were looking and laughing at him, a 24 pound ball went through the flour just above his head, throwing staves, heads, hoops, and flour over him. He

jumped up and ran sideways into a wet ditch of two
feet of water screaming "O Lord, O Lord!" Some
of the men ran to pull him out, supposing he would
drown. I told them to let him lie there, he was out
of the range of the fire, and not worth pulling out.[18]

In the early morning hours of the 3rd, a company of British
gunners with a six pound cannon, a 5½ inch howitzer, and
a mortar of the same size,[19] crossed the Maumee and erected
a gun battery along a ravine some 300 yards east of the fort.
Opening fire upon the American garrison at 10:00 in the morning, the new gun emplacement could potentially allow the
British to place the fort under a devastating cross-fire. Captain Wood had anticipated this action by the enemy, however,
and short traverses had been ordered erected within the camp.
These new traverses intersected at right angles to those built
at the battle's start, making the camp's interior reasonably
secure from the possibility of enfilade fire from the sides.[20]

When the defenders became aware of the new British position two or three of the fort's 18 pound cannon were brought
to bear on the enemy emplacement, silencing it for a brief time.
The full potential of the enemy battery, however, was never
realized, owing in part to the poor aim of the British gunners
manning the pieces, for:

> The person who was employed with the howitzer
> seemed either a friend or possessed of very little skill
> in his profession, for notwithstanding he was but
> about three or four hundred yards distant from the
> camp, yet not more than one out of four or five
> shells thrown ever came within the lines. It was the
> opinion of many of our men that he certainly must
> be a friend and felt for our situation.[21]

At noon on the 4th, Captain Oliver, who had been sent to
General Clay with orders for the Kentucky Brigade to advance
to the Rapids, returned to the camp with news that he had
found Clay at Fort Winchester.

The Kentucky commander had been aware of the British attack prior to meeting with Harrison's messenger. Hearing un-
confirmed reports of the British assault while moving down

the Auglaize River to Defiance, Clay had dispatched a young Kentuckian, Leslie Combs, to proceed in advance of the main body of reinforcements and advise Harrison of the approaching column. Traveling with four others and guided by Black Fish, a Shawnee warrior, Combs and his party left Defiance for Fort Meigs by canoe. Safely passing through the Rapids, Combs and his party came under heavy musket fire from Indians on the shore as his vessel neared the American outpost. Two of the Kentuckians with Combs fell wounded, one mortally. Unable to continue, Black Fish turned the canoe to the opposite shore where the unharmed members of the expedition made good their escape.[22]

Despite Combs' failure to reach the American garrison, Clay and the Kentucky reinforcements were at present less than five miles from Fort Meigs at the head of the Rapids, prepared to make the final descent to the stockade. Harrison now had the means to deliver a decisive blow against the British. Harrison's plan was to split the 1,200 men of Clay's command into two parties, landing 800 men on the north bank where they would attack the British batteries, spike the cannon, and recross the river to the safety of the stockade. The remaining 400 would land on the south shore upriver from the fort and fight their way to the camp, dispersing the Indians harrassing the garrison on the west. While Clay's men executed their assignments, a detachment from the fort would attack and silence the British gun emplacements on the east.[23]

Before dawn on the 5th, Harrison dispatched Captain Hamilton and two others upriver to Clay to inform the Kentuckian of his instructions. Hamilton reached Clay before sunrise. The emotional strain of the dangerous journey through enemy lines, however, had caused at least one of the messengers to arrive "panic struck," and much confused. Clay, nonetheless, was correctly informed of Harrison's intentions.[24]

Clay divided his force according to Harrison's instructions, and being the senior officer, placed himself in charge of the detachment ordered to land on the south bank. Colonel William Dudley, the second in command, led the expedition to the north shore.[25] Just before dawn, Clay began the two-pronged assault in the midst of a heavy rain. The entire column descended the rapids in eighteen flatboats, stockaded with pucheons set on end and loopholes notched into the sides for the delivery of musket volleys.[26] Clay commanded the last six vessels, Dudley the first twelve. With Dudley was the guide who had become confused.[27]

Though the current was swift, Dudley managed to execute a safe landing, undetected by the British. Once aground, Dudley divided his command into three parallel columns. Dudley personally led the right, the center was commanded by Major John Morrison, and the left by Major James Shelby, son of the Kentucky Governor. A small detachment commanded by Captain Leslie Combs flanked the expedition to the far left.[28] The heavy rain had caused many of the men's weapons to become waterlogged, so Dudley decided that the charge was to be made with bayonets only.[29] Although Dudley was aware that his orders were to attack the British batteries, spike the guns and return across the river to Fort Meigs, these instructions, due either to an oversight on Dudley's part or to the "confusion" of the guide sent by Harrison, were incorrectly passed to the men of his command. Many of the troops now marching with the Colonel were either unsure of their objectives, or believed that they were to attack the batteries and continue the assault until they had reached the main British camp.[30] This failure of communication and the resulting confusion among the landing party was to prove disastrous to the mission.

Dudley's column descended upon the unsuspecting British unobserved, and after raising a "horrid Indian yell," charged the batteries, routed the gun crews, spiked eleven cannon, and cut down the British colors, all without the loss of a single man.[31] The men within Fort Meigs who had watched Dudley's progress with suspense and apprehension leaped upon the stockade walls, loudly cheering the Kentuckians' success, while the men on the north bank responded with huzzas of their own, one of the Americans within the camp writing that:

> We mounted the picketting and reechoed their cheers from the garrison. My God Crittenden, what a moment! My soul seemed as if it would burst its bounds. Most willingly would I have yielded it to my God and parted from all on Earth that is dear to man to have crowned the glory of this moment with (a) successful time. Alas! The fates had not so declared.[32]

As the men in Dudley's column lingered at the captured British position, Shelby's command moved to a point between the fallen batteries and Fort Miami, encountering a party of Indians, the beginning of a major relief force moving up from the British camp. Unaware that they were to retreat across the Maumee, a hotly contested skirmish broke out as the Kentucky column continued the charge.

Dudley, at the fallen British batteries, heard the musket reports of Shelby's men and realized that his comrades were in great peril. Caught now between duty and honor, Dudley's dilemma was whether to obey orders, abandon his friends to the enemy and retreat across the river with the troops in the immediate vicinity, or to form his men and march to Shelby's relief. Honor prevailed. The Colonel marshalled his command and moved off into the woods.

As the combined American columns advanced against the British and Indians, the enemy forces would pause, engage the Kentuckians briefly, and then fall back to repeat the maneuver again. Each charge of the American force would carry them further from Fort Meigs and deeper into a steadily strengthening British counter-attack.[33] Observing the developments on the north bank from a vantage point on one of the fort's batteries, Harrison immediately perceived the mortal danger which Dudley and his men were in. Angrily yelling across the river ordering Dudley to retreat and getting no response, he offered a 1,000 dollar reward to any man who would brave the river crossing and compel the Kentuckian to return to the fort. A Lieutenant Campbell made the attempt, but he was turned back by the swift current.[34]

The Kentucky assault which had met with quick success against the unsuspecting, unprepared gun emplacements now faltered and disintegrated in the face of stiff, determined British resistance. Pursuing Indian skirmishers to their front, the Americans were soon flanked on each side and eventually surrounded by enemy troops. Though the sortie was contested for nearly three hours, the attackers had no chance of escape as the heavy rain had caused many of the troops to enter the battle with either wet weapons or ammunition that was incapable of firing. In addition, virtually the entire expedition was exhausted from fighting in the wet, marshy ground.[35] Enthusiasm turned to concern and then to panic as the assault became a retreat and retreat a route. Dudley's attempt to save his command had not succeeded and had cost him his life along with Major Morrison and about fifty of his men. Of the 800 soldiers to land with Dudley, nearly 650 were captured or killed. Less than 150 of the expedition managed to escape to Fort Meigs.[36]

As the American assault terminated and the battle ended, the Kentuckians surrendered and the British soldiers and their Indian allies collected their prisoners. One of the expedition later recalled that:

> ...The course, broad command, "ground your arms, surrender," pronounced by British officers banish(ed) all hope of successful resistance. "Damn your eyes, ground your arms or you will be slain," brought me hastily to my senses. Down went gun, off came knapsack, to hastily disappear beneath the mud and water, then ankle deep where I stood, and with my full weight I aided their exit from further service, pressing them as deeply into the mud as possible.[37]

While the prisoners were herded together and marched off towards Fort Miami, many were robbed of valuables and stripped of their clothing by the Indians. The procession neared the British stronghold, and the tempo and severity of physical abuse increased. While the Americans moved towards the British gates, the Indians formed a gauntlet, "clubbing and tomahawking all they could of the terror-struck prisoners."[38] Entering the fort, the survivors were once again assailed by the Indians, who fired their muskets into their midst at random and continued to tomahawk and scalp the fallen victims. Though the massacre was occuring under the eyes of several British officers, Proctor among them, no move was made on their part to stop the killing. A single British soldier by the name of Russell attempted to grab an American from his attacker and was shot through the heart.[39]

Only the appearance of Tecumseh himself put a stop to the slaughter. Upon hearing of the massacre in progress, the Shawnee Chief immediately returned to the British fort. Entering the camp and,

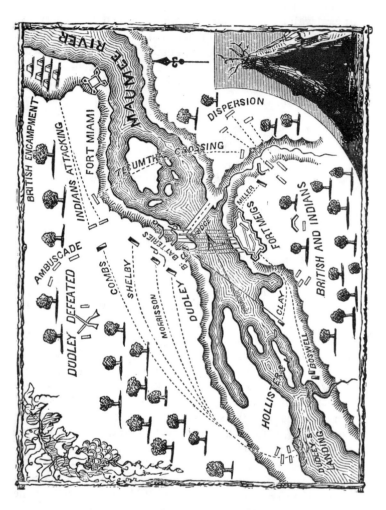

First Siege of Fort Meigs

Drawing his tomahawk and scalping knife, he ran
in between the Americans and Indians, brandishing
them with the fury of a madman, daring any of the
hundreds who surrounded him to attempt to murder
another prisoner. They all appeared confused and
immediately desisted. His mind appeared rent with
passion, and he exclaimed, almost with tears in his
eyes, "Oh what will become of my Indians!" He
then demanded in an authoritative tone, where
Proctor was, and nervously casting his eyes about
and seeing that officer at a short distance, he sternly
inquired why he had not put a stop to the inhumane
massacre. "Sir," said Proctor, "Your Indians cannot be commanded." "Begone!" retorted
Tecumseh in the greatest disdain. "You are unfit
to command, go and put on petticoats."[40]

The killing was stopped, but not before nearly forty
Americans had fallen. The surviving captives were gathered
together and taken to the British gunboats moored in the river
and placed in the holds. Within a few hours the fallen British
gun emplacements had been remanned and the pieces placed
back into service.[41]

Though Dudley had met with failure on the north bank, the
400 troops commanded by Green Clay succeeded in safely landing on the south shore and driving the Indians from the fort's
west. Moving down the Maumee Clay attempted to land his
entire detachment together, but the river's fast flow separated
Clay's flatboat from the others. As the main contingent
grounded themselves opposite Dudley's landing, Clay managed
to reach the shore somewhat upstream.[42] Unlike Dudley's landing, Clay's advance was opposed from the start.

As the flatboats approached the bank, they received a brisk
fire from Indians on the beach. The fire was returned by means
of musket volleys fired from behind the boat's stockading, killing at least one Indian and sending the others away.[43] Landing
safely, Clay regrouped and, after leaving seven soldiers to guard
the boats, began the march to the fort. Although meeting with
occasional skimishers, the column was not challenged with a
unified resistance. Musket and cannon fire from the fort cleared
the way and, assisted with reinforcements from the garrison,

the column entered the stockade without incident.

Once within the walls of Fort Meigs, the Kentucky detachment was met by Harrison. He ordered that they re-form with a small force from the garrison, leave the fort over the same route from which they had just arrived, re-engage the enemy and return once more. This maneuver was executed twice. Each time the Indians were pushed further from the stockade.[44] The landing and subsequent charges had cost the Americans forty-five wounded, one of whom was Clay who had fallen into an open trench upon entering the fort, injuring his leg. Three of the seven men guarding the landing craft were killed, apparently the only deaths to occur among the Kentuckians landing on the south bank.[45]

Harrison also ordered that an attack be made on the British batteries to his east to coincide with the assault of the Kentucky troops. Assembling a force consisting of regulars and militia troops from Ohio and Kentucky 350 strong, Harrison placed Colonel John Miller of the 19th Infantry in command. Advancing along a small ravine to the south of the fort, the detachment silently approached the British position, each man under strict instructions not to fire until the command was given. As the column left the protective shelter of the ravine, it came under heavy fire from the British and Indians. Forced to halt and reform his lines less than fifty yards from the enemy guns, Miller at last gave the order to attack, and a concentrated, lethal volley poured into the British emplacement.

Miller's men charged the British guns taking the battery, capturing the crew, and spiking the cannon tubes. Beginning the retreat to the fort, the Kentucky contingent of Miller's group encountered stiff opposition from two Canadian Militia Companies amounting to 130 men and nearly 300 Indians. The Kentuckians, led by Captain William Sebree, held their ground until reinforced and the entire expedition, with forty-two prisoners, returned to the garrison. Though victorious, Miller's success had cost the expedition over a third of their number in casualties, thirty dead and ninety wounded.[46]

As the action surrounding Miller's charge subsided, all grew quiet on both shores of the river. Late in the afternoon a cannon volley from the British batteries across the Maumee caught the Americans unaware, killing several, but for all intents and purposes, the fighting on the 5th had ended. Early in the evening, Proctor sent an envoy to Harrison demanding the surrender of the garrison. Harrison, reinforced, reasonably well provisioned, and having sustained few casualties within the stockade, declined to capitulate, though an agreement was reached to negotiate the exchange of prisoners.

The following day no fighting took place, though white flags from both camps passed between the lines. It was agreed that all the regulars captured throughout the preceeding day would be mutually exchanged at once. The captive remnants of Dudley's command would be boated to near the mouth of the Huron River where they would be paroled. Once released they would be free to go, but not to fight again unless they were formally exchanged for British soldiers being held prisoner.[47]

During the lull in the battle, two British officers made use of the occasion to stroll through the Indian encampment to the rear of Fort Miami. Here they encountered:

> A spectacle (which) was at once of the most ludicrous and revolting nature. In various directions were lying the trunks and boxes taken in the boats of the American division, and the plunderers were busily occupied in displaying their riches, carefully examining each article, and attempting to define its use. Several were decked out in the uniforms of the officers, and although embarrassed in the last degree in their movements, and dragging with difficulty the heavy military boots with which their legs were for the first time covered, strutted forth much to the admiration of their less fortunate comrades. Some were habited in plain clothes, others had their bodies clad with clean white shirts, contrasting in no ordinary manner with the swarthiness of their skins, all wore some articles of decoration, and their tents were ornamented with saddles, bridles, rifles, daggers, swords, pistols, many of which were handsomely mounted and of curious workmanship. Such was the ridiculous part of the picture, but mingled with these, and in various directions were to be seen the scalps of the slain drying in the sun, stained on the fleshy side with vermillion dyes, and dangling in the air as they hung suspended from poles to

which they were attached, together with hoops of various sizes, on which were stretched portions of human skin taken from various parts of the human body, principally the hand and foot, and yet covered with the nails of those parts, while scattered along the ground were visible the members from which they had been separated, and serving as nutrient to the wolf-dogs by which the savages were accompanied.

As we continued to advance into the heart of the encampment, a scene of a more disgusting nature arrested our attention. Stopping at the entrance to a tent occupied by the Minoumini tribe we observed them seated around a large fire, over which was suspended a kettle containing their meal. Each warrior had a piece of string hanging over the edge of the vessel, and to this was suspended a food, which it will be presumed we heard not without loathing, consisted of a part of an American. Any expression of our feelings, as we declined the invitation they gave us to join in their repast, would have been resented by the Indians without much ceremony. We had, therefore, the prudence to excuse ourselves under the plea that we had already taken our food, and we hastened to remove from a sight so revolting to humanity.[48]

To attack and reduce Fort Meigs had proved a more formidable task than Proctor had at first anticipated. Prepared now to resume the siege, Proctor found that he could not. The Indians under Tecumseh had believed the British claims that the siege would be a short one, but seeing it extended over days with no end in sight they became deeply dissatisfied. Satiated with the plunder taken from Dudley's men and unwilling to wait any longer, they rapidly began to drift away. To the members of the Canadian Militia accompanying Proctor, the expedition to the Maumee Rapids had come at a particularly inopportune time. Many of them were farmers and the possibility of famine loomed oppressively before them and their families if they were not permitted to return home at once to plant their crops.[49] Like the Indians, many of the militia brigades simply evaporated.

The ranks of the regulars, too, were seriously weakened. Though battle related casualties had been light, dysentery and the ague had raged through the British camp depleting the number of battle ready effectives. On the 7th, Proctor received a dispatch advising him that Fort York had fallen and the General believed, though incorrectly, that a large force of Americans was at present moving westward to cut off his return route to Fort Malden. His forces depleted, his provisions nearly exhausted, and expecting a major American counter-attack, Proctor was compelled to abandon the siege.[50]

Throughout the 7th and 8th, all remained quiet upon the battle ground. The pause was a welcomed respite to the Americans who watched the British as they made the final preparations to withdraw. The suspicion, however, that the enemy's actions were a ruse, "some deep plan to annoy us," remained with the defenders.[51]

Before dawn on the 9th, two deserters from the British camp swam the river and entered the garrison, bringing the news that most of the enemy cannon had been loaded upon the British gunboats during the night, and that the expedition was ready to depart. As the first light of morning broke over the river valley, the British were completing the loading of supplies and beginning to board their men. At 10:00 a.m., the British colors were struck to the accompaniment of American cheers and the last enemy soldier walked aboard the waiting vessels. As the flotilla embarked for Amherstburg, a cannon volley was sent from the fort. The volley was returned in kind from the departing ships, killing several of the Americans who had mounted the stockade to witness the retreat.[52]

The siege was over. At 12:00 noon, the cannons of Fort Meigs fired a salute three times around the stockade.[53] Throughout the days of bombardment, nearly 1,700 shot and shell had been thrown at the American position. Remarkably, only seventy to eighty men within the fort had been killed, and about 189 were wounded.[54] One of the wounded, however, was Amos Stoddard, who had been injured on the first day of the siege while commanding the fort's grand battery. Suffering with tetanus as a result of his injuries, Stoddard died on the morning of the 11th. In addition to those killed or wounded within the fort were the fifty or so killed and over 600 captured during Dudley's assault on the north shore batteries.

Among the British troops Proctor recorded a total of fourteen killed, forty-seven wounded and forty-one taken prisoner, although there is some evidence that indicates he may have discounted his actual casualties in his official report.[55] Proctor's figures also do not include information concerning Indian dead and wounded, the actual number of which cannot be determined.[56]

The first thoughts of the garrison were for the wounded, many of whom had been lying in the trenches on "rails barely sufficient to keep them out of the water, which in many places, from the bleeding of the wounded, had the appearance of puddles of blood." The ordnance was removed from the blockhouses along the stockade wall and tents and marquees erected at their entrances, converting these buildings into temporary medical facilities for the injured. The fort, however, was woefully short of trained medical personnel and supplies. Indeed, the shortage of qualified physicians caused Harrison to report to Secretary of War Armstrong that:

> The Surgeon of the 19th Regt. has been represented
> to me, by several Medical and other respectable
> characters upon whom I can rely, as being a perfect
> quack, alike destitute of talents, medical experience,
> and education.[57]

In addition, the garrison's supply of fresh meat and vegetables, necessary to nurse the sick back to health, was virtually gone. Though the wounded were cared for as much as the circumstances permitted, many suffered greatly. A visitor to one of the hospitals observed an officer of the Engineers laying on a bed in the corner.

> He had rendered much service from the beginning
> of the war, and his courage was unquestionable. But
> now, in consequence of the irritation of his nerves
> by the roar of artillery, the bursting of bombs, the
> pain of his wounds, and his feverish condition, he
> had become as timid and as peevish as a child, and
> constantly apprehensive of being torn to pieces by
> a cannon ball . . . Stretched on a pallet lay Captain

Jack Shore . . . At the commencement of the can-
nonading, he had solicited a station in one of the
principle batteries . . . One of the guns was dismounted by a shot from the enemy, and an iron
splinter pierced his leg. It was immediately extracted. The wound was considered unimportant,
and was slightly bandaged. However, in a few hours
it became distressingly painful, and he retired to the
hospital. He was now suffering in the last stage of
lock-jaw. In his spasmodic agony, the smoke of his
torment literally rose in a mist from his blanket. We
gave him a hot bath, but to no purpose; he sank
in death, lamented by all.[58]

Parties from the fort reconnoitered the battle ground and
the site of the British encampment, finding and returning with
a great deal of abandoned equipment including unused shot
and shell. Other details crossed the river to discover and bury
the dead, and forty-five, including Dudley and several of his
officers, were interred on the north bank.[59] Other parties began
the arduous chore of repairing the stockade, blockhouses and
magazines of the garrison.

The exhilaration and excitement of combat soon gave way
to exhaustion and the emotional strain of the preceding days
became apparent. As the camp's dead were gathered and committed with full honors, a sense of melancholy and depression
shrouded the garrison. One of those assigned to a burial detail
wrote:

We interred between forty-five and fifty . . . I knew
many of the men we found, and God avert my eyes
from such another scene to the end of time. It was
weeks, Crittenden, before nature reasserted itself.
Everything like mental powers seemed to wither and
die, night after night did the horrid spectacle op-
press me.[60]

Yet beneath this despondency was the realization that the
Americans had persevered in the face of a worthy and respected
adversary. As the scars of the wounded healed and the breaches
of the stockade were repaired, the routines of camplife

reasserted a sense of order and purpose. On May 17, ten days after the British had departed, Captain Cushing noted in his diary:

> Fine weather this morning, my men in high spirits, fish plenty, no want of provisions. All that is wanting to have things complete is a little whiskey.[61]

Notes for Chapter III

[1] **Michigan Pioneer and Historical Collections in 40 Volumes**, Vol. 15, "Embarkation Return of the Western Army Commanded by Brig. General Proctor on An Expedition To The Miamis, Amherstburg, 23d April, 1813," p. 276.

[2] "Charles Marvin to Joseph H. Larwill, April 27, 1813," personal letter (Larwill Family Papers, Archives-Library Collection, Ohio Historical Society).

[3] **Michigan Pioneer and Historical Collections**, Vol. 15, "Major Chambers to Secretary Freer, Amherstburg, 13th May, 1813," pp. 289-91.

[4] "Marvin to Larwill, April 27, 1813"; Harlow Lindley, ed., **Fort Meigs and the War of 1812, Orderly Book of Cushing's Company, 2nd U. S. Artillery April, 1813 - February 1814, and Personal Diary of Captain Daniel Cushing October, 1812 - July, 1813**, (Columbus: Ohio Historical Society, 1975), p. 115; **Niles Weekly Register**, June 12, 1813.

[5] Lindley, **Fort Meigs**, p. 116; Richard C. Knopf, ed., **Document Transcriptions of The War of 1812 In The Northwest**, Vol. 7, pt. 2, **Letters To The Secretary of War 1813 Relating To The War of 1812 In The Northwest**, (Columbus: Ohio Historical Society, 1961), "Harrison to Armstrong, April 28, 1813," p. 64.

[6] Knopf, **Letters To The Secretary of War 1813**, pt. 2, "Shelby to Armstrong, April 18, 1813," pp. 47-48.

[7] Benson J. Lossing, **The Pictorial Fieldbook of the War of 1812**, (Somersworth: New Hampshire Publishing Company, 1976), p. 478.

[8] Lindley, **Fort Meigs**, p. 116; Robert B. Boehm and Randall L. Buchman, eds., **Journal of the Northwestern Campaign of 1812 - 1813 under Major General Wm. H. Harrison by Bvt. Lieut.-Colonel Eleazer D. Wood, Captain Corps of Engineers, U. S. Army**, (Defiance: Defiance College Press, 1975), p. 19.

[9] John Richardson, **Richardson's War of 1812; with notes and a Life of the Author by Alexander Clark Casselman**, (Toronto: Historical Publishing Company, 1902), p. 148.

[10] Lindley, **Fort Meigs**, p. 116.

[11] Boehm and Buchman, **Wood's Journal**, p. 20.

[12] "To His Excellency Green Clay, Affidavit of Abner Young, July 9, 1813," (Green Clay Papers, Burton Historical Collection, Detroit Public Library).

[13] Lindley, **Fort Meigs**, p. 116; Captain John H. Neibaum, "The Pittsburgh Blues, The Story of Fort Meigs," **Western Pennsylvania Historical Magazine** 4 (1921): 175-85.

[14] Alfred M. Lorrain, **The Helm, The Sword, And The Cross: A Life Narrative**, (Cincinnati: Poe & Hitchcock, 1862), pp. 129-30; see also, James P. Averill, **Fort Meigs, A Condensed History of The Most Important Military Point in the Northwest, Together With Scenes and Incidents connected with the Sieges of 1813, and a Minute Description of the Old Fort and its Surroundings as they now Appear**, (Toledo: Blade Printing and Paper Company, 1886), p.22

[15] Neil E. Salsich, "The Siege of Fort Meigs, Year 1813, An Eye-Witness Account by Colonel Alexander Bourne," **Northwest Ohio Quarterly** 17 (1945): 151.

[16] Averill, **Fort Meigs, A Condensed History**, pp. 22-23; Boehm and Buchman, **Wood's Journal**, pp. 20-21.

[17] Boehm and Buchman, **Wood's Journal**, p. 22.

[18] Salsich, "Bourne's Journal," p. 153.

[19] **Michigan Pioneer and Historical Collections**, Vol. 15, "Chambers to Freer, May 13, 1813," pp. 289-91.

[20] Boehm and Buchman, **Wood's Journal**, p. 21.

[21] Ibid.

[22] Lossing, **Fieldbook**, pp. 480-81.

[23] Lossing, **Fieldbook**, p. 485; Lindley, **Fort Meigs**, p. 117.

[24] "J. H. Hawkins, Aid de Camp to Crittenden, August, 1813," personal letter, (Clay Papers, Archives-Library Collection, Ohio Historical Society); Knopf, **Letters To The Secretary of War 1813**, pt. 2, "Clay to Harrison, May 9, 1813," pp. 97-98.

[25] Lossing, **Fieldbook**, p. 485.

[26] "Hawkins to Crittenden, August, 1813."

[27] Ibid.

[28] Leslie Combs, **Col. Wm. Dudley's Defeat Opposite Fort Meigs, May 5, 1813, Official Report From Captain Leslie Combs to General Green Clay, Printed for William Dodge**, (Cincinnati: Spiller & Gates, Printers, 1869), p. 1.

[29] Thomas Christian, "Campaign of 1813 on the Ohio River, Sortie at Fort Meigs, May, 1813," **Kentucky Historical Society Register** 67 (1969): 262.

[30] "William Johnson to Mary Johnson, May 11, 1813," personal letter, (Private collection, photo dupulicate and transcrip-

tion, Fort Meigs Collection); Lossing, **Fieldbook,** p. 486;
Combs, **Official Report,** p. 6; Robert B. McAfee, **History of
the Late War in the Western Country,** (Bowling Green:
Historical Publications Company, 1919), p. 291; James Green,
"Journal of Ensign William Schillenger, A Soldier of the War
of 1812," **Ohio Archaeological and Historical Quarterly** 41
(1932): 71; Lieutenant Joseph Rogers Underwood, "Dudley's
Defeat & Running The Gauntlet," (Unpublished manuscript,
Western Kentucky University), p. 4.

[31] Lossing, **Fieldbook,** p. 486.

[32] "Hawkins to Crittenden, August, 1813."

[33] Combs, **Official Report,** p. 6.

[34] Earl A. Saliers, "The Siege of Fort Meigs," **Ohio Archaeological and Historical Quarterly** 18 (1909): 532; Lossing,
Fieldbook, p. 486.

[35] Combs, **Official Report,** p. 6.

[36] John Gellner, ed., "A Common Soldier's Account,
Shadrack Byfield, a Private in the 41st Foot, Fights Humbly,
Patiently, and Bravely, From Detroit to Lundy's Lane,"
Recollections of the War of 1812, Canadian Heritage Series,
Vol. 4, (Toronto: Baxter Publishing Company, 1964), pp. 9-14.

[37] Thomas Christian, "Campaign of 1813," pp. 263-64.

[38] Ibid., p. 264; Underwood, "Dudley's Defeat," pp. 10-11.

[39] Lossing, **Fieldbook,** p. 489; Richardson, **Richardson's
War of 1812,** p. 154; Knopf, **Letters To The Secretary of War
1813,** pt. 2, "Harrison to Armstrong, May 18, 1813," pp.
114-16. Another British officer who witnessed the event recalled
that the murdered British soldier's name was Paddy Kassil,
[Major Peter Chambers?], "The War in Canada 1812 - 1814,"
Public Archives of Canada, MG-40-0-1B.

[40] Averill, **Fort Meigs, A Condensed History**, p. 27; Richard C. Knopf, ed., **Document Transcriptions of the War of 1812 In The Northwest**, vol. 5, pt. 2, **The National Intelligencer Reports The War of 1812 In The Northwest**, (Columbus: Ohio Historical Society, 1961), "Zanesville, O., May 19, (1813)," pp. 119-20. This text of Tecumseh's rebuke to his warriors, though found in many sources, is almost certainly apocryphal. Leslie Combs, one of the American captives at Fort Miami recounting the episode in a less romantic, though undoubtedly more accurate account, indicates that Tecumseh addressed his Indians in the Shawnee language. Combs relates that Tecumseh "came striding briskly into the midst of the surrounding savages, and taking his position on the highest point of the wall made a brief but most emphatic address. (I) could not understand a word of what he said, but it seemed to receive the general assent of the Indians . . . and (I) knew from his manner that he was on the side of mercy." **Narrative Life of General Leslie Combs; Embracing Incidents In The History of the War of 1812**, (Washington: American Whig Review Office, 1852), p. 12.

[41] "Capt. Jo. H. Hawkins to His Excellency Isaac Shelby, Gov. of Kentucky, May 6, 1813," personal letter, (Miscel. Manuscripts Collection, Cincinnati Historical Society).

[42] Lossing, **Fieldbook**, p. 487.

[43] "Hawkins to Crittenden, August, 1813."

[44] "James Love to Eliza C. Tunstal, May 10, 1813," personal letter, (Thomas Love Papers, The Filson Club).

[45] "Hawkins to Crittenden, August, 1813"; Knopf, **Letters To The Secretary of War 1813**, pt. 2, "Clay to Harrison, May 9, 1813," pp. 97-98.

[46] Emmanuel Hallaman, "The British Invasions of Ohio - 1813," **Papers on the War of 1812 in the Northwest**, No. 1, (Columbus: Anthony Wayne Parkboard & The Ohio State Museum, 1958), p. 11.

47 Knopf, **Letters To The Secretary of War 1813**, pt. 2, "An Agreement for the Exchange of Prisoners made between Brigadier General Proctor Commanding His Britanic Majesty's Forces on the Miamis and Major General W. H. Harrison Commanding the North Western Army of the United States, May 7, 1813," p. 90.

48 Henry Howe, **Historical Collections of Ohio in Three Volumes**, Vol. 3, (Columbus: Henry Howe & Son, 1891), p. 575; Richardson, **Richardson's War of 1812**, pp. 158-59; see also Underwood, "Dudley's Defeat," pp. 15-16.

49 **Michigan Pioneer and Historical Collections, Vol. 15.** "Statement of Militia Captains, Camp Miamis, 6th May, 1813," p. 280.

50 Richardson, **Richardson's War of 1812**, pp. 160-61.

51 Lindley, **Fort Meigs**, p. 118.

52 Ibid., p. 119; Lossing, **Fieldbook**, p. 489; Knopf, **The National Intelligencer Reports**, pt. 2, "Minutes of the principle occurences which have taken place during the siege of Fort Meigs, from the 25th of April to the 9th day of May; taken down by a volunteer in the fort, June 7, 1813," pp. 127-30; **Michigan Pioneer and Historical Collections**, Vol. 15, "Brig. General Proctor to Sir George Prevost, Sandwich, May 14, 1813," pp. 293-96.

53 Lindley, **Fort Meigs**, p. 119.

54 Knopf, **The National Intelligencer Reports**, pt. 2, "Copy of a dispatch from Major-General William Henry Harrison, to the Secretary of War, May 13, 1813," pp. 109-10.

55 Alec R. Gilpin, **The War of 1812 In The Old Northwest**, (East Lansing: The Michigan State University Press, 1958), p. 118.

56 **Michigan Pioneer and Historical Collections**, Vol. 15, "Return of Killed, Missing, Wounded and Prisoners under the

Command of Brig. General Proctor at the Battle fought at the Miamis, 5th May, 1813,'' p. 277.

[57] Knopf, **Letters To The Secretary of War 1813**, pt. 2, "Harrison to Armstrong, May 19, 1813," pp. 119-20.

[58] Lorrain, **The Helm, The Sword, and the Cross**, pp. 138-39; see also Boehm and Buchman, **Wood's Journal**, pp. 27-28.

[59] Lindley, **Fort Meigs**, pp. 118-19.

[60] "Hawkins to Crittenden, August, 1813"; see also Boehm and Buchman, **Wood's Journal**, p. 28.

[61] Lindley, **Fort Meigs**, p. 121.

Chapter 4

On May the 10th, the men of the garrison dug themselves out of their trenches and were greeted by "the first fair day we have experienced in eight days."[1] While the wounded were tended and the repairs to the fort had begun, Harrison assessed the situation. It was true that Fort Meigs had withstood the British attack and the invasion had been turned back. Yet the failure of Dudley's attack with its attendant high cost in casualties and prisoners had removed the claim of unqualified success from Harrison's reach. Nonetheless, when the commanding General addressed his men he chose to do in commendatory terms.

Speaking to the troops of the fort in the General Orders of May 6, Harrison noted that he could not "pass by the opportunity which the events of yesterday afforded of expressing to the troops his high sense of distinguished valor which they manifested in each of the three severe conflicts in which they were engaged."[2] Harrison continued, praising the various companies of militia, volunteers, and regulars who had responded with honor during the conflict. When he commented on the actions of Dudley's command on the north bank, however, his tone turned to one of censure. "It is truly painful to reflect that this operation so eminently successful in the commencement should have been brought to an unfortunate issue by temerity and disobedience of our troops." Echoing these sentiments in the General Orders of May 9, Harrison noted that:

> It rarely occurs that a General has to complain of
> the excessive ardor of his men, yet such appears
> always to be the case whenever the Kentucky Militia
> are engaged. It is indeed the source of all their
> misfortunes, they appear to think that valor alone
> can accomplish everything . . . such temerity,
> although not so disgraceful is scarcely less fatal than
> cowardice.[3]

With the repairs to the fort well under way and the garrison in reasonably good order, Harrison left the Rapids on May the 12th, assigning command of the fort to Brigadier General Green Clay. Traveling to Lower Sandusky through the Black Swamp, Harrison met Governor Meigs who was personally leading a 1,000 man column of Ohio Volunteers destined to relieve Fort Meigs.[4] With the siege over, unable to adequately provision and supply such a large force, and encumbered by War Office regulations limiting the use of volunteers and militia, Harrison was unable to use the new troops at his disposal. Still wary of the possibility of a second attack by the British though, he dispatched several militia detachments to continue to Cleveland and ordered that two other companies remain at Lower Sandusky.[5]

Speaking to the remainder of the reinforcements, Harrison praised their courage and the vigor with which they had responded to the call to arms. After expressing his "warmest gratitude," he reluctantly ordered that the rest of the expedition disband and return home.[6]

At Fort Meigs, the capable leadership of Green Clay brought the garrison to a position of strength. Traverses were leveled, blockhouses and store houses rebuilt, stockading and powder magazines repaired. To increase the effectiveness of the fortification against a second attack, Clay ordered that two new gun emplacements be erected. Designed by Gratiot, one gun position was placed along the previously battery-less west wall. The other was positioned on a redoubt near the northeast corner of the stockade.[7] Reconnaissance patrols sent to survey the battle field retrieved a large quantity of abandoned British equipment and so many cannon balls that the fort was now actually better supplied than when the siege had started.

Though the garrison was well armed and equipped, the bombardment had seriously damaged several of the store houses that contained the fort's beef, pork and flour. Furthermore, much of the camp's remaining provisions had been ruined by the incessant rains and dampness. The rations on hand, supplemented by regular shipments of beef, flour and produce, however, were adequate to provide for the troops and a critical shortage of food was avoided.

As the repairs and alterations to the fort were completed and the daily activities of the garrison settled back to the routine, the months of May, June and July provided the troops with increased opportunities for recreation and leisure. Captain Daniel Cushing set out a garden of lettuce, radishes, sage, mint, onions and peas, and on May the 17th noted in his diary:

> I took sail in a small canoe this morning and caught
> 62 white bass that weigh about one pound each,
> caught them with a hook and line baited with a red
> rag.[8]

Spring was arriving in the Maumee Valley and much to Clay's dismay, as the temperature moderated, so did the rigid discipline of the camp. Lacking the inherent emotional tension of impending attack and the inspiration of combat with which to reign in his troops, Clay fought a losing battle against his own men as they bent, broke or "forgot" the post's regulations. Clay, unlike Leftwich, was determined not to have his authority undermined and asserted his control. Court martials became frequent, and while the violations and infractions of the camp's rules were, by and large, less serious than those brought to trial prior to the siege, they were more numerous.

Throughout this period the General Orders were filled with increasingly explicit commands defining the proper appearance of the troops, noting the correct time and duration of drill, and listing the conditions under which bathing, swimming, laundry and fishing would be allowed to take place. Indeed, by midsummer it was necessary to chastise the civilian population of the garrison as well, the General Orders of August the 1st noting that:

Brigadier General Green Clay

> Any married woman who has or shall abandon her
> husband and be found strolling about camp or lodg-
> ing in the tent of other men shall be drummed out
> of camp.[9]

Though for the most part the soldier's transgressions posed
no serious or long lasting threat to the security and safety of
the camp, one particularly serious problem proved insidious.
The areas of the fort which had been designated as living
quarters for the troops greatly suffered from an inattention
to simple cleanliness. In many of these areas garbage, trash
and refuse piled high on the ground. Latrines were often im-
properly placed or constructed and the most basic of rules
regarding their use and upkeep went unenforced.[10]

Clay railed his men about the unhygenic squalor in which
they lived with almost predictable regularity. Ordering that
these areas be regularly policed, Clay demanded immediate action and instituted severe penalties for those who refused to
comply. Although Clay met with some success, for the most
part his orders went unheeded. Undoubtedly exacerbated by
the unsanitary conditions of the camp, a mid-spring outbreak
of measles and mumps felled many of the men, cutting the effective fighting force of the approximately 2,100 man garrison
nearly in half.[11]

The spring calm was broken on June 20. That morning, two
men arriving from Detroit brought with them the news that
the forces of Tecumseh and the British were again massed and
poised for a second assault agains the Rapids.[12] The information returned a sense of sobriety and determination to the garrison. Before the day was done, parties had been sent from
the fort to level the remains of the British batteries across the
river and to cut the brush from around the stockade's
perimeter.

Gun carriages were repaired and cannon remounted and
placed in readiness as the garrison prepared for its defense.
Clay also sent expresses informing General Harrison of the in-
telligence and ordered that the commandants of Upper and
Lower Sandusky, Fort Findlay, Fort McArthur, and the
Blockhouse on the Portage River ready their encampments for
an attack. To bolster the number of battle-ready troops at the
Rapids, orders were sent for the mounted troops of Colonel

Richard M. Johnson, presently at Fort Winchester, to proceed to Fort Meigs as quickly as possible.[13]

In the days that followed, every available soldier contributed to the strengthening of the site. One of the participants wrote:

> This day all the effective men within the garrison are on guard or on fatigue, repairing the batteries, clearing off the woods around the camp, cutting, hauling, and placing arbonets in front of all the batteries. Every man appears to be working for his own safety.[14]

Harrison was at Franklinton when news of the British plans reached him. Convinced that a second invasion was imminent he believed, though, that the British would not once again attack the Maumee Rapids, but instead would thrust towards either Lower Sandusky, Cleveland, or Erie, Pennsylvania.[15] Determined to strengthen his position along the northwest, Harrison immediately sent units of the 17th and 24th Infantry stationed at Upper Sandusky and Colonel Ball's Squadron of Dragoons stationed at Franklinton, to Lower Sandusky.[16]

Briefly detained at Franklinton, Harrison soon overtook the 24th Regiment on its way to the northwest on the 26th of June. After selecting those who would continue on a forced march, he proceeded to Fort Meigs, arriving there on the 28th. Having heard no reports concerning the movements of the British since the 20th, he dispatched a detail of Colonel Johnson's Mounted Regiment to scout the Frenchtown region. Returning the next day, Johnson reported that he had searched the area, and although he had heard several reports of minor Indian expeditions aimed against Fort Meigs, he had not seen any evidence of a concerted enemy attack.[17]

Fort Meigs was now in good repair, adequately manned and provisioned. With no apparent sign of the British in the vicinity, Harrison felt no need to linger at the Rapids. Leaving the garrison on July 1, the General traveled on to Lower Sandusky to inspect the facilities there and to plan for the completion of Fort Stephenson.[18]

The garrison at Fort Meigs was awakened at dawn on the 4th of July by the firing of thirteen cannon in honor of the nation's independence. The day was to be one of celebration.

As the troops were paraded for morning inspection, General Clay announced that every man reported fit for duty was to receive an extra gill of whiskey in his daily ration and then cancelled all fatigue duties for the day. Continuing, Clay then dissolved all court martials underway in camp and ordered the release of all those under sentence or confinement, stating:

> The General is induced to use this lenity alone from the consideration of this ever memorable day, and flatters himself that in the future the soldiers under his command will better appreciate their liberty by a steady adherance to duty and prompt compliance to the orders of their officers, by which alone they are worthy to enjoy the blessings of that Liberty and Independence, the only real legacy left us by our Fathers.[19]

Early in the afternoon, the troops were once again assembled near the grand battery, and a National Salute of eighteen rounds was fired from the post's heavy guns. As the soldiers were dismissed, the garrison's officers adjourned to continue the festivities under a large arbor that had been specially constructed for the occasion. The officers, joined by the fifes, drums, flutes, clarinets, violins, and timbrels of the Band of Independent Volunteers, offered eighteen toasts, each followed by a patriotic song played by the musicians. Presiding over the assembly, Clay delivered the first toast. As the band played "Yankee Doodle," Clay proclaimed:

> The day of our Freedom, its blessings to all the world! It should admonish our ancient and inveterate enemy Great Britain, that what was purchased by the blood of our fathers, their sons will be ever ready to maintain.

The ceremony continued and one observer noted that "Every eye proclaimed the Fourth of July as the day most dear to America, (the day) most animating to the patriot's bosom."[20]

The first weeks of July passed and the fort became the scene of frequent harassment by small parties of raiding Indians. Early in the month, a mounted party of eighteen men from the fort was attacked as they were on their way to the head of the Rapids to escort a shipment of flour destined for the garrison. Moving towards the waiting flatboats, the detail was fired upon by three Indians who had lain in ambush. Lieutenant Elijah Craig, who commanded the Americans, called a retreat at once and was obeyed by all but three of his men. One of the soldiers, though, pursued the attackers some two hundred yards into the woods where he shot and killed one of the Indians.

When Craig returned to the fort and made his report, Clay was outraged at his cowardly conduct and ordered that he be arrested and stripped of his command. When the soldier who had pursued the Indian, George Wiant, returned carrying the fallen Indian's scalp and rifle, Clay promoted him to the rank of Ensign on the spot and presented him with the finest sword in the fort's arsenal.[21]

Although such occurrences kept the post vigilant, it was generally assumed by mid-month that the earlier reports of a second British invasion were false. Nonetheless, Clay continued to send out scouts, drill his men, and to pay strict attention to the security of the camp. On the 20th of July, Lieutenant Peters of the Artillery, who was returning from Lower Sandusky, was surprised and attacked by a large force of Indians. Peters and his party escaped to the fort unharmed, but by late evening the sails of British ships could be clearly seen from the stockade walls. The enemy had returned. Once more Fort Meigs was besieged.

The Indians participating in the first assault upon Fort Meigs had been bitterly disappointed in the outcome.[22] Since spring they had been applying ever mounting pressure on Proctor to launch a second attack to reduce the American fortification. Proctor, however, was having problems of his own as his men, equipment, artillery, and provisions were being diverted to strengthen the forces of Captain R. H. Barclay, the British naval commander on Lake Erie.

Proctor and Barclay had together attempted to draw a strong force of regulars from the east to be used in a decisive preemptive strike against the American naval yards at Erie, Pennsylvania. Hoping, as with the first invasion, to combine British troops with a strong detachment of Indian warriors, Proctor had permitted the British Indian Agent at Detroit, Colonel Robert Dickson, to assemble the needed Indians in mid-spring.[23]

Dickson had succeeded admirably. By late June nearly 1,400 braves from the western tribes had been gathered at Detroit and Michilimackinac. An observer in Detroit at the time wrote that:

> It was in June, 1813, that I saw one of the wildest and most grand, and beautiful Indian sights that I ever beheld. Colonel Dickson of the British Indian Department had been upon the upper Mississippi and Green Bay Country collecting Indians to fight for them. About twelve or fifteen hundred warriors came down the river one very beautiful morning, all in birch canoes, with the British flag flying, singing their war songs, and as they approached the headquarters of General Proctor at Sandwich, at a given signal they commenced firing their guns and turned the bows of their canoes towards the Sandwich, or Canada, shore, landing in beautiful order, one after the other, the line of canoes nearly reached across the Detroit River. They were met upon landing by a party of the 41st and 39th British Regulars with their bands and colors flying, the Indians forming in squads of fifty, each squad painted differently all over their bodies as they were nearly in a nude state. They thus advanced escorted by the troops, dancing and singing their war dance until they reached the house of General Proctor, where a speech was made to the General in which they said all they asked was to get a chance to fight the long knives at Fort Meigs, that the Fort was not built so strong but that they could not climb it like a squirrel. All they wanted was to show their British Father the bravery of the Indian Warrior.[24]

With the Indians, however, came more headaches for Proctor.[25] The Indians and their families were consuming over 1,400 rations daily.[26] Already severely strapped for food and supplies, he could ill afford to hold the Indians in reserve for any extended period of time. Proctor had to act immediately if he was to use the Indian force at his disposal. Yet, without the help of reinforcements of regulars from the east, he was powerless to move against the American naval yards.

In mid-July, with his repeated requests for additional men and rations curtly refused, Proctor proposed a strike against the ill defended American camp at Lower Sandusky. The Indians, however, would not be swayed. Demanding to attack Fort Meigs a second time, they forced Proctor to acquiesce to their wishes. On July the 20th, therefore, Proctor, with between three and four thousand Indian warriors, but only about 350 regulars and a few light field pieces, again embarked for the Maumee Rapids.

Though surprised at the sudden appearance of the British, Clay was prepared. With the fortification in an excellent state of repair, well manned, armed, and equipped, and with enough rations on hand to last through December, he was confident of the garrison's ability to withstand the assault. Expecting another extended artillery siege, Clay ordered that the traverses again be thrown up the length of the stockade's interior and that the men sleep with their arms and ammunition at the ready. Addressing his command, Clay stated:

> The enemy having again presented themselves, it will be necessary to repel them with every exertion in our power. (The General) does not deem it necessary to appeal to the feelings of the troops composing this garrison to excite them to the most noble deed of valor in the approaching contest. The preservation of the lives of helpless thousands, the honor of the American character and arms, depends on the maintenance of this post. No other excitements than those are wanting to animate the bosoms of all those who now have an opportunity to share the glory of defeating the enemy.[27]

As during the first siege, the British unloaded their troops and established their base camp on the north shore near the remains of Fort Miami. The Indians crossed the river to surround the fort.[28] Before sunrise on the 21st, a picket guard sent to patrol the fort's exterior was ambushed and about a half dozen of its men were killed or taken prisoner.[29] Throughout the remainder of the day and the three that followed, the battle took on a predictable pattern. The Indians would approach the stockade close enough to fire into the fort, only to be driven away by the musket fire and occasional cannon volley of the Americans.

Within the garrison the men lived in comparative safety as the enemy was unable to inflict any serious casualties among the defenders. Indeed, although the men of the garrison were ostensibly in the middle of a pitched battle, the mood in the camp was calm, almost casual, one of the defenders noting that:

> Never did I expect to see men grow so indifferent to the sound of bullets. At home, if a gun is fired at a man a mile off, it is a great concern to the neighborhood. Here, if a man has his glass of grog shattered as he passes it to his lips, it is treated with derision.[30]

Early on the morning of the 24th, the British were observed taking all of their men, equipment, and boats to the south bank where they then moved to positions emcompassing the southern flank of the fort. Within the garrison the enemy's maneuvering was interpreted to be the preliminary step to a massive full scale attack against the south wall. Once again Clay addressed his men, stating:

> The movements of the enemy indicate an attack of some description. To fight is to conquer, to abandon our posts is to suffer disgrace and the most shocking massacre. The General cannot believe there is an individual in the garrison whose breast would not burn with indignation at the idea of the American character being tarnished in our hands. Should, however, there be anyone so lost to every sense of honor as to shamefully abandon his post, or order a retreat without proper authority, he shall suffer death.[31]

The remainder of the day and evening passed without incident, and by 2:00 a.m. the following morning every man was at the stockade wall, each with two or three loaded muskets at his side, waiting to meet the anticipated assault. To the bafflement of the Americans the charge never came. As dawn broke, the British and Indians pursued the same line of tactics as they previously had, appearing at the edge of the woods to fire their small arms at the American camp and then dispersing in the face of rifle and cannon fire from the fort.

Early in the day Captain Joseph McCune, a messenger who had been in contact with General Harrison, slipped into the fort. According to McCune, Harrison had been advised of the siege and was collecting a large force of reinforcements at Lower Sandusky. In addition, Governor Meigs was also calling out the Ohio Militia. If needed, claimed McCune, the fort could expect to be relieved within two or three days.[32]

At about 4:00 in the afternoon, the sound of heavy gunfire was suddenly heard about a mile from the fort on the Sandusky Road which led from the southwest angle of the stockade. Above the noise of battle could distinctly be heard the sound of the Indians. Appearing to approach and then recede from the fort, the conflict always remained out of sight. By all indications it seemed that an unexpected column of reinforcements for the garrison had come under attack and was meeting with fierce resistance as it attempted to fight its way to the safety of the fort.[33]

Calling a hastily convened council of his senior officers, Clay sought their advice. Many of the officers present vigorously protested that the General should open the gates and permit a detachment from the fort to go to the aid of the supposed reinforcements. It was Clay alone among the officers, however, who had personally commanded a detachment that had become the victim of rash action in the face of determined British and Indian opposition. During the first siege he had been the one to lead the Kentucky brigade to the fort and had seen Dudley's brigade destroyed on the opposite shore. Unable to explain the action taking place along the south flank, he was nonetheless confident that the report he had received earlier in the day regarding the location of Harrison's and Meigs' reinforcements was accurate. Although, at present, American reinforcements were being marshalled, and perhaps even now might be on the way to Fort Meigs, the relief columns were not in the immediate vicinity.

Clay supposed that the action taking place to the south was nothing more than a ruse, a sham intended to draw the

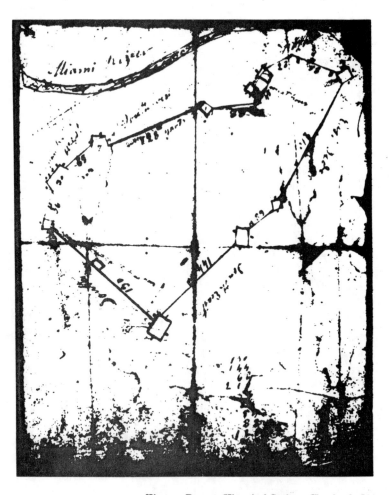

Plat Map of Fort Meigs
Plat map of Fort Meigs drawn April 1, 1813.
Perhaps the earliest surviving rendering of Fort
Meigs, this map was sketched nearly a month before
the fortification was completed. The drawer has in-
dicated the distances between the features of the
stockade, and has noted on the map's reverse that
the measurements were estimated by pacing them off.

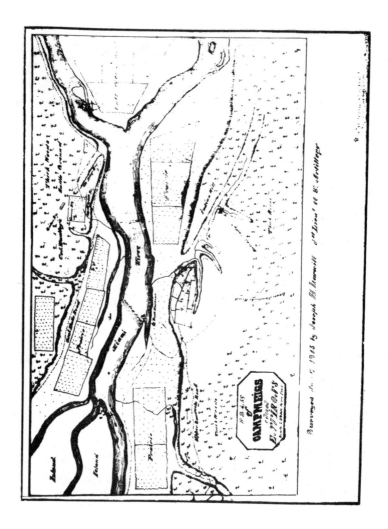

Larwill Map

Map of Fort Meigs drawn on July 19, 1813 by Joseph Larwill showing the position of the four British artillery batteries employed during the first siege on the north shore of the Maumee (Miami) River, and the site of the fifth battery erected on the south bank to the east of the stockade.

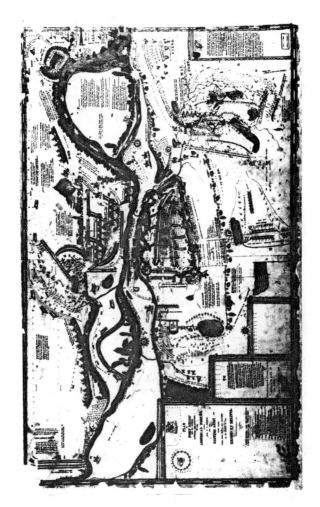

Sebree's Plan of Fort Meigs
One of the great pieces of American folk art to come
out of the Northwestern Campaigns of the War of
1812, this map, drawn to 3 different scales by
William Sebree c. 1814, shows the simultanious ex-
ecution of events associated with both sieges. Captain
Sebree commanded Sebree's Company of Infantry,
Kentucky Militia, from March 6, 1813 through
September 6, 1813.

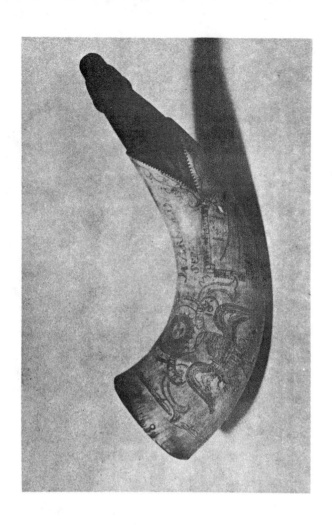

Fort Meigs Powder Horn
Powder horn attributed to Francis Tansel made for
James Arnold, dated September 12, 1813. Arnold
and Tansel both served with the Kentucky Militia at
Fort Meigs. Arnold arrived at the fort with the Ken-
tucky Brigade commanded by Green Clay in May of
1813, and served as a private in Captain Peter
Dudley's Company of Infantry. He was discharged
from duty on September 9, 1813. Tansel enlisted as a
private in Captain John Duvall's Company of Infan-
try on May 28, 1813, and was discharged on
September 28, 1813.

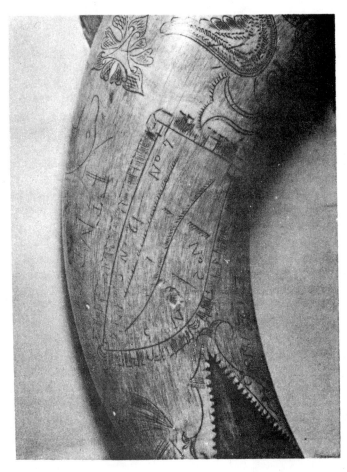

Powder Horn Detail
Detail of the Tansel powder horn showing an
engraved map of Fort Meigs.

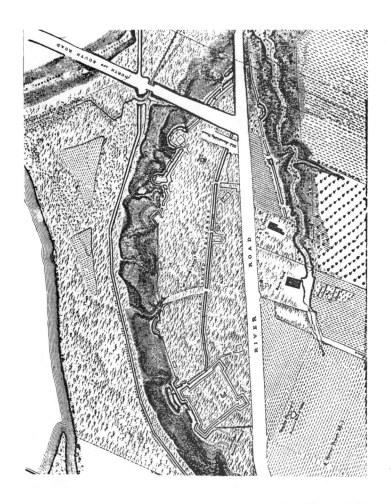

U.S. Army Corps of Engineers Map, 1888, Detail
Detail from a U.S. Army Corps of Engineers survey
of the site of Fort Meigs, 1888. The outlines of the
smaller stockade, erected after the 10 acre fort was
demolished in September, 1813 can clearly be seen in
the northwest corner.

defenders from the safety of the stockade. If a strong detachment from the fort could be lured from the garrison, ambushed and defeated, the fort would then be weakened enough to be vulnerable to a full-scale assault. Challenged with bitter disagreement from his officers, Clay counseled caution and restraint. The gates would not be opened. No detachment was to be sent to the rescue.[34]

Within an hour of the beginning of the alleged "battle", a storm, "the heaviest thunder shower that ever I experienced," according to one of the Americans, blew over the battle field. As the rains began, the firing ceased. The next day few of the enemy were seen, and by the 28th, the eighth day of the siege, the British and their allies had vanished.[35] Clay was vindicated. Unable to take the fortification by either force or deception, the British had left the field. The siege was over.[36]

Losses to the Americans had been light, the only serious casualties being the half dozen or so men of the picket guard killed or captured during the first day of battle.[37] Likewise, the British suffered no serious loss during the engagement. Damaged, however, was Proctor's prestige among the Indians as he, for the second time, had demonstrated his inability to capture the American fortification.

Still bending to the pressure of his Indian allies and hoping to salvage his reputation among them, Proctor turned his army to the poorly defended post at Lower Sandusky, Fort Stephenson. Recently completed, Fort Stephenson was presently manned with only 160 troops commanded by Major George Croghan. With an overwhelmingly superior force at his disposal, Proctor sensed an easy victory at the head of the Sandusky River.

Harrison, who had been informed of the enemy's movements, regarded the post as untenable and sent orders to Croghan to abandon the fort and retreat. The General's message, though, arrived at Fort Stephenson only after the vanguard of Proctor's Indians had surrounded the garrison. Croghan felt that he had no choice but to stay and fight.

The main body of British troops arrived at Lower Sandusky on July 31.[38] After disembarking, Proctor sent an envoy, Colonel Elliot, under a flag of truce to demand the surrender of the post. Croghan's intermediary, Ensign Shipp, declined and, as he attempted to walk back to the stockade, was accosted

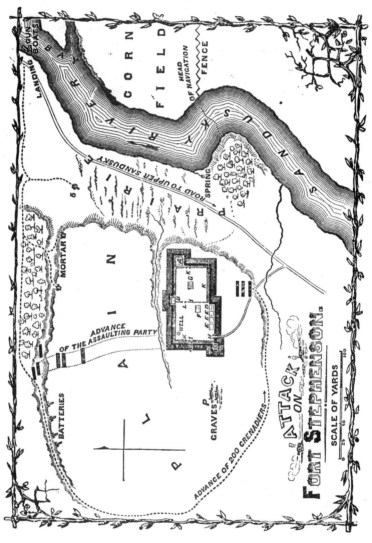

Lossing, Ohio Historical Society

Attack on Fort Stephenson

Buffalo Gazette, Extra,

Wednesday Morning, Aug. 11, 6 A. M.

SIEGE of FORT MEIGS RAISED, and ATTACK on LOWER SANDUSKY by the BRITISH.

The two following extracts of letters were received in a printed hand bill by the western mail, at 12 last night : We soon expect to have more particulars.

—

From the Erie Centinel, August 8.
Extract of a letter from Maj. General Harrison to Com. Perry, dated Head-Quarters, Seneca Towns, 9 miles from Lower Sandusky, 4th August, 1813.
" The seige of Fort Meigs was abandoned by the enemy on the 27th ult. On the evening of the 1st inst. they appeared before the post of Lower Sandusky, and about 5 o'clock P. M. of the 2d attempted to carry it by storm. In this rash attempt they were repulsed with great loss, two officers (a Lt. Colonel by brevet, and a Lieutenant) with about 50 men, penetrated to the ditch. where they were all killed and wounded but two or three, who were sheltered by the dead bodies by which they were covered. We have 26 prisoners. Gen. Proctor retreated down the Sandusky river, with the utmost precipitation."

Copy of a letter from Major J. O. Fallon to Capt. R. D. Richardson at this place, dated Seneca Towns, August 4th, 1813.
The General has written Capt. Perry as explicitly as I could now to you, about Croghan's glorious success over the British and Indians, in their assault upon his post. He was attacked simultaneously on three different points, on all of which the enemy suffered prodigiously. I yesterday counted in the ditch and on its brink 27 that were there killed, it is generally believed that more than that number of killed were taken off. The fort had been bombarded and cannonaded one night and day by 5 six's and one howitzer.

The killed, wounded and prisoners are supposed to exceed two hundred. Gens. M'Arthur and Cass are here.
Your friend,
JOHN O. FALLON.
Gov. Meigs is close at hand with an almost incalculable number of militia.—Tecumseh with 2000 Indians, it is said, is yet this side the Miami. J. O. F.

Buffalo Gazette, Extra
Broadside issued on August 11, 1813 describing the British withdrawal from Fort Meigs on July 27, 1813, and the American victory at Fort Stephenson.

by an Indian who tried to grab the American's sword. The Indian was restrained by a British officer, but at the height of the altercation Croghan mounted the ramparts and yelled, "Shipp, come in and we will blow them all to Hell!" [39]

Early on August 1, Proctor began to bombard the post with his light artillery and howitzers from the gunboats. The light pieces were ineffective, and by late afternoon the following day he had decided to attempt an assault. As the British force approached the walls, all guns within the fort opened fire, and the post's lone artillery piece, a six pounder called "Old Bess," raked the ditch. For the British it was a catastrophe. The Indians dispersed at the first sound of American cannon. The British troops caught helplessly in the ditch had no chance. Ninety-six British soldiers, nearly a third of the regulars attached to the expedition, were killed, wounded or captured. Decimated with casualties and abandoned by his allies, Proctor called the retreat, boarded his vessels and returned to Canada. [40] The second invasion of the Northwest had been a failure. Proctor's withdrawal marked the end of the British presence in Ohio during the War of 1812.

Throughout the summer months, the workers at the American naval yards at Erie, Pennsylvania had been busily laboring to complete the American fleet destined for use on Lake Erie. Construction had commenced in October of the previous year, and in August the building of the ships was finished. Taking to the lake the first week of August, the fleet was commanded by Commodore Oliver Hazard Perry. Sailing to the northwest, Perry cruised the Western Basin towards Fort Malden, effectively imposing a blockade around the British stronghold and exacerbating an already critical shortage of provisions within the enemy camp.

The nine vessel American squadron was a formidable force. Two nearly identical brigs of 480 tons, the **Lawrence** and the **Niagara,** mounted eighteen thirty-two pound carronades and two long twelve pound cannon. Of the remaining smaller vessels the **Ariel** mounted four guns, the **Caledonia** three, and the **Scorpian** two guns and two swivels. Smaller yet, the **Trippe, Tigress, Porcupine,** and **Ohio** carried one gun apiece. Joined by nearly one hundred experienced sailors from the east and one hundred Kentucky marksmen detached from Harrison's army in mid-month, the flotilla established its headquarters near Put-In-Bay, where it continued to harass British supply boats and awaited the opportunity to engage the British fleet.

On September the 9th, Captain Barclay and the British navy accepted the challenge and sailed from the Detroit River to meet the Americans. The six vessel British fleet, though smaller than the American force, had a slight advantage in the number of guns that it mounted. Barclay's two largest brigs, the **Detroit** and the **Queen Charlotte**, carried nineteen and seventeen guns respectively. The **Lady Prevost** boasted thirteen cannon, the **Hunter** eight. These large vessels were accompanied by two smaller gunboats, the **Little Belt** mounting two guns, and the **Chippeway** carrying eight. Perry was well aware of the size and composition of the British force. Barclay commanded a distinct advantage only in his ability to utilize his more numerous long range cannon. Perry's plan of attack, therefore, was to engage the British as close and as quickly as possible, thereby allowing the American commander to unleash his thirty-two pound carronades.

At daybreak on September the 10th, American lookouts spotted the approach of Barclay's sails on the horizon. Sailing from the island at once, Perry confronted the British at 11:00 a.m., with the wind working in Barclay's favor. Suddenly, as the two forces converged, the wind shifted giving Perry the advantage. Just before noon the guns of the **Detroit** opened fire. The engagement was begun.

Proceeding according to his previous strategy, Perry, in his flagship **Lawrence**, moved in quickly to challenge the British at close quarters. Barclay, in the **Detroit**, delivered a withering fire, and was soon joined by the **Queen Charlotte**, who also brought her guns to bear upon the American flagship. The **Lawrence** was cut to ribbons. Nearly eighty percent of her crew was killed or wounded, though Perry remained unhurt. The Americans, however, had extracted a severe penalty. The British sustained heavy casualties and Barclay himself was gravely wounded.

With the **Lawrence** virtually shot from beneath him, Perry transferred headquarters from the disabled vessel to aboard the **Niagara** and renewed the battle. Sweeping towards the **Detroit** and the **Queen Charlotte**, who had become entangled

Battle of Lake Erie
*Commodore Oliver Hazard Perry transfers his flag
from the disabled Lawrence to the Niagara during
the Battle of Lake Erie.*

in each other's rigging, Perry raked both ships with devastating broadsides from his thirty-two pounders. The **Caledonia** moved in to support the **Niagara** and Perry's smaller gunboats closed to join the fray.

British opposition disintegrated. The **Detroit** and **Queen Charlotte** surrendered, followed quickly by the **Hunter** and **Lady Prevost**. The **Chippeway** and **Little Belt** attempted to flee but were soon caught by the American gunboats. The defeat of the British flotilla was absolute. Perry had won complete control of Lake Erie.[41]

With the British expelled from the Ohio country and the American Navy firmly in control of Lake Erie, Harrison's long awaited opportunity for a decisive invasion of Canada was now at hand. Pursuing a plan of attack approved by Secretary of War John Armstrong the previous March, Harrison had begun in August to gradually accumulate troops from many of the garrisons in the Northwest, including a substantial number from Fort Meigs,[42] in preparation for the attack.

With many of the men and much of the provisions and equipment stored at Fort Meigs being brought forward to support the anticipated assault, the large post at the foot of the Maumee Rapids was no longer needed. In mid-August Clay and Harrison had agreed to reduce the size of Fort Meigs. Much of the existing structure was to be burned and dismantled. Replacing the large fortification would be a smaller stockade roughly fifty yards square, incorporating the existing blockhouse in the northwest corner of the larger fort.

New stockading consisting of fourteen foot pickets set four feet in the ground would surround the rebuilt fortification. On the outside of the post, earth was to be mounded up to within five feet of the stockade's top, and a steep sided ditch six feet deep and five feet across encircled the position. Blockhouses were constructed at each corner of the four sided fortification, each placed to allow cannon from within to completely rake the ditch if necessary. Within the post, permanent barracks and store houses were erected to house and supply the reduced garrison.[43] On August 21, wagon drivers were procured to begin the new construction, and by September 5, the new fort was nearly completed and most of the older structure demolished.[44]

Duncan McArthur

On September 11, two Indian scouts who had been at the River Raisin returned to camp reporting that they had heard a heavy gunfire on Lake Erie and that they supposed the sound was the American Navy engaging the British fleet.[45] Brigadier General Duncan McArthur of the Ohio Militia, who had assumed command of the fort on August 27, immediately dispatched a fifteen man party down river to determine the results of the battle. His fears, however, were not alleviated until the 13th when an official dispatch from Harrison informed him of Perry's victory.[46] With Harrison's dispatch were orders for the Ohio General to advance to the Portage River with all but eighty of the men stationed at the post.

At the Portage, McArthur and the men of Fort Meigs joined with the other troops assembled by Harrison. Once massed at the Portage, Harrison's army was carried by Perry's fleet to Put-In-Bay on September 20, and from there to Middle Sister Island on the 25th. On the 26th, Harrison joined Perry on the **Ariel** and set sail for the Detroit River to reconnoiter his approach to Amherstburg. Returning to Middle Sister Island that evening satisfied that his anticipated corridor of attack was secure, the General issued orders for the invasion to proceed the next morning.[47]

At 3:00 in the afternoon the following day, Perry's fleet landed the invading Americans some three miles below Amherstburg. The British, however, were nowhere to be seen, and Harrison's force entered the town unopposed. Perry's naval victory had placed Proctor in an increasingly untenable position. Though his army was large, he did not have the supplies on hand to adequately provision his troops, nor were reinforcements to be forthcoming. His plan, therefore, was to withdraw up the Thames River to a more strategically defensible position and there engage the Americans.[48] The sight of Perry's **Ariel** off the mouth of the Detroit on the 26th, however, was Proctor's first indication that the anticipated invasion was underway. Leaving the vicinity in great haste, the fleeing British army was but a short distance in front of Harrison, destroying equipment, provisions and bridges as it retreated.

After lingering in Amherstburg until elements from the mounted regiment of Colonel Richard Johnson had secured the town of Detroit, Harrison renewed the pursuit on October 2. In their haste, the retreating British had neglected to destroy

Large Swamp

Small Swamp

MAIN BODY OF INDIANS

BRITISH AND INDIANS

TECUNTHA FELL

PROCTOR

CANNON

BRITISH

THOMPSON

SPIES

JOHNSON

SPIES

R.M.JOHNSON

J.JOHNSON

PAUL AND INDIANS

THAMES

RIVER

HARRISON

SHELBY

Desha's Division

CALDWELL

TROTTER

KING

CHILE

SIMRALL

ALLEN

DETROIT

TO.

ROAD

BATTLE OF THE THAMES.

Lossing, Ohio Historical Society

Battle of the Thames

several key bridges beyond Sandwich. As a consequence, the American army quickly reached the mouth of the Thames before sunset that evening. Proceeding vigorously along the south bank of the Thames, the invaders captured a small work detail of British soldiers on the 3rd, and encountered slight Indian resistance on the 4th. Later in the day Harrison's men neared McGregor's Mill, a store house for British grain. Torched by the British, the ruins of the mill still smoldered as the invading army passed the site. Camping for the night at Bowles Farm, some five miles above Chatham, the army discovered two burning British vessels and the partially destroyed remains of a brewery containing a large supply of muskets and artillery. On the 5th, Harrison continued the chase, capturing a British wagon conductor three miles below Moravian Town. The captive related that the British army was formed and ready for battle but a short distance ahead. The pursuit was over. Harrison had reached his adversary.

The British forces were deployed in two divisions waiting to meet the American attack. One group formed in rather loose order across the road leading to Moravian Town with the Thames to their left and a narrow swamp to their right. The second division prepared in two lines to the right of the first force, the narrow swamp to their left. On their right stretched a large swamp and at its fringe waited Tecumseh and his Indians.

Harrison ordered his mounted troops to engage the British infantry and commanded his infantry to attack the Indians in the swamp. The charge was sounded and the cry of "Remember the Raisin!" was raised by the Americans as the attack commenced. The battle was brief, spirited and decisive. The British infantry, outnumbered and poorly supplied, fired only three volleys before capitulating. The Indians, however, continued to fight tenaciously, but the death of Tecumseh brought an end to the battle an hour and a half after the British line had surrendered.[49] Proctor, who had fled the melee at the first sign of British collapse, managed to escape the American onslaught. Nonetheless, the British army had been dealt a blow from which it would not recover. Detroit was repatriated, the British swept from Lake Erie, Proctor was defeated, and Tecumseh was dead. The American victory on the Thames foreshadowed the conclusion of military operations in the Northwest theater during the War of 1812.

Death of Tecumseh
*Print dating from the 1830's depicting the death of
Tecumseh at the hands of a mounted Kentucky
soldier, allegedly Richard M. Johnson.*

At the Maumee Rapids the much reduced Fort Meigs continued to be manned by a small detachment of Ohio Militia. Garrisoned until after the war's end, the fort served as a supply link for men and equipment moving along the Maumee River. In May of 1815, the men of the post received orders to be brought forward to Detroit. One last time Lieutenant Almon Gibbs assembled and paraded the forty men of his command. For the final time the troops at Fort Meigs were reviewed, the flag lowered and the colors retired. At the end of the ceremony the soldiers marched to the schooner **Blacksnake** waiting at the docks below. Built to defend Ohio in a war that was over, and used to supply an army that no longer existed, Fort Meigs had served its purpose. With quiet dignity the post was abandoned.

Notes for Chapter IV

[1] Harlow Lindley, ed., **Fort Meigs and the War of 1812, Orderly Book of Cushing's Company 2nd U. S. Artillery April, 1813 - February, 1814, and Personal Diary of Captain Daniel Cushing October, 1812 - July, 1813**, (Columbus: Ohio Historical Society, 1975), p. 119.

[2] Ibid., p. 21.

[3] Ibid., pp. 24-26.

[4] Richard C. Knopf, ed., **Document Transcriptions of The War of 1812 In The Northwest, Vol. 7, pt. 2, Letters To The Secretary of War 1813 Relating To The War of 1812 In The Northwest**, (Columbus: Ohio Historical Society, 1961), "R J Meigs to Gen Cass, May 3, 1813," p. 79.

[5] Knopf, **Letters To The Secretary of War 1813**, pt.2, "Harrison to Armstrong, May 18, 1813," pp. 114-16.

[6] Logan Esary, ed., **Messages and Letters of William Henry Harrison**, Vol. II, (Indianapolis: Indiana Historical Commission, 1922-1964), p. 449; Richard C. Knopf, ed., **Document Transcriptions of The War of 1812 In The Northwest**, Vol. 3, **Thomas Worthington and The War of 1812**, (Columbus: Ohio Historical Society, 1957), "McArthur to Worthington, May 22, 1813," pp. 183-84.

[7] Lindley, **Fort Meigs**, pp. 51-52.

[8] Ibid., p. 121.

[9] Ibid., p. 54.

[10] "Police Reports, Camp Meigs," (Green Clay Papers, Burton Historical Collection, Detroit Public Library).

[11] Lindley, **Fort Meigs**, p. 123.

[12] Knopf, **Thomas Worthington and The War of 1812**, "John Miller to Genl. Thos. Worthington, June 24, 1813," p. 204; Knopf, **Letters To The Secretary of War 1813**, pt. 2, "Clay to Harrison, June 20, 1813," pp. 179-80; Richard C. Knopf, ed., **Document Transcriptions of The War of 1812 In The Northwest**, Vol. 2, **Return Jonathon Meigs Jr. and The War of 1812**, (Columbus: Ohio Historical Society, 1957), "Clay to Meigs, June 20, 1813," pp. 232-33.

[13] Lindley, **Fort Meigs**, pp. 33-34; Knopf, **Letters To The Secretary of War 1813**, pt. 2, "Clay to Harrison, June 20, 1813," pp. 179-80.

[14] Lindley, **Fort Meigs**, p. 128.

[15] Richard C. Knopf, ed., **Document Transcriptions of The War of 1812 In The Northwest**, Vol. 5, pt. 2, **The National Intelligencer Reports The War of 1812 In The Northwest**, (Columbus: Ohio Historical Society, 1958), "Extract of a letter from General Harrison to Governor Meigs, June 23, 1813," p. 133.

[16] Knopf, **Letters To The Secretary of War 1813**, pt. 2, "Harrison to Armstrong, June 23, 1813," p. 183.

[17] Robert B. McAfee, **History of the Late War in the Western Country,** (Bowling Green: Historical Publications Company, 1919), pp. 329-31.

[18] Ibid.

[19] Lindley, **Fort Meigs**, pp. 132, 142-43.

[20] Knopf, **The National Intelligencer Reports**, pt. 2, "Fourth of July In Camp, Camp Meigs, July 4, 1813," pp. 141-42.

[21] McAfee, **History of the Late War**, pp. 341-42.

[22] Knopf, **Letters To The Secretary of War 1813**, pt. 2, "Harrison to Armstrong, June 8, 1813," pp. 163-64.

[23] **Michigan Pioneers and Historical Collections In 40 Volumes**, Vol. 15, "Captain Roberts to Secretary Freer, 23 June, 1813," p. 322.

[24] Richard J. Wright, ed., **The John Hunt Memoirs, Early Years of The Maumee Valley Basin, 1812-1835**, (Maumee: Maumee Valley Historical Society, 1979), p. 25.

[25] Milo M. Quaife, ed., **The John Askin Papers**, Vol. II, 1796-1820, (Detroit: Detroit Library Commission, 1931), pp. 761-63.

[26] **Michigan Pioneer and Historical Collections**, Vol. 15, "Campaign of 1813," p. 321.

[27] Lindley, **Fort Meigs**, pp. 48-49.

[28] "Remarks on Board the Schooner **Nancy**, Transport at anchor in the river Miami in the month of July, 1813," Public Archives of Canada, MG-19-C1.

[29] Lindley, **Fort Meigs**, p. 143; Knopf, **Letters To The Secretary of War 1813**, pt. 3, "Harrison to Armstrong, July 23, 1813," p. 32.

[30] "J. H. Hawkins, Aid de Camp to Crittenden, August, 1813," personal letter, (Clay Papers, Archives-Library Collection, Ohio Historical Society).

[31] Lindley, **Fort Meigs**, p. 50.

[32] Ibid., p. 136; Knopf, **Letters To The Secretary of War 1813**, pt. 3, "Harrison to Armstrong, July 28, 1813," pp. 41-42.

[33] McAfee, **History of the Late War**, pp. 345-46; John Gellner ed., "A Common Soldier's Account, Shadrack Byfield, A Private in the 41st Foot, Fights Humbly, Patiently, and Bravely, From Detroit to Lundy's Lane," **Recollections of the War of 1812, Canadian Heritage Series**, Vol. 4, (Toronto: Baxter Publishing Company, 1964), p. 19.

[34] Benson Lossing, **The Pictorial Fieldbook of the War of 1812,** (Somersworth: New Hampshire Publishing Company, 1976), pp. 498-99.

[35] Lindley, **Fort Meigs**, p. 136; Knopf, **Letters To The Secretary of War 1813**, pt. 3, "Harrison to Armstrong, August 1, 1813," pp. 47-48.

[36] Knopf, **The National Intelligencer Reports**, pt. 2, "Chillicothe, August 3, (1813)," p. 145; "An Interesting Journal of the Second Siege of Fort Meigs by an Officer of respectability at that Place, September 14, 1813," pp. 183-85; John Niebaum, "The Pittsburgh Blues, The Story of Fort Meigs," **Western Pennsylvania Historical Magazine** 4 (1921): 175-85.

[37] Lindley, **Fort Meigs**, p. 136.

[38] "Remarks on Board the Schooner **Nancy**."

[39] Lossing, **Fieldbook**, p. 501.

[40] Knopf, **The National Intelligencer Reports**, pt. 2, "Copy of a letter from Major General Harrison to the Secretary of War, August 4, 1813," pp. 146-47; **Michigan Pioneer and Historical Collections**, Vol. 15, "Brig. Gen. Proctor to Sir George Prevost, August 9, 1813," pp. 347-50; Gellner, "Shadrack Byfield," pp. 21-23; [Major Peter Chambers?], "The War in Canada 1812 - 1814," Public Archives of Canada, MG-40-0-B.

[41] Knopf, **The National Intelligencer Reports**, pt. 2, "Copy of a letter from Commodore Perry to the Secretary of the Navy, September 13, 1813," pp. 193-94; "Extract of a letter from a Correspondent, on board the U. S. brig **Hunter**, September 24, 1813," pp. 232-33; "Extract of a letter from a Naval Officer now at Erie to his Friend in this City, October 7, 1813," p. 235. A transcription of Captain Barclay's subsequent court-martial and several detailed accounts by American seamen taking part in the action are found in Richard C. Knopf, ed., **Document Transcriptions of the War of 1812 In The Northwest**, Vol. 4, **Anecdotes of the Lake Erie Area**, (Columbus: Ohio Historical Society, 1957); see also [Chambers?], "The War in Canada."

[42] Knopf, **Letters To The Secretary of War 1813**, pt. 3, "Anderson to Armstrong, October 10, 1813," pp. 86-87; Knopf, **The National Intelligencer Reports**, pt. 2, "Copy of a letter from Commodore Perry to the Secretary of the Navy, September 20, 1813," p. 209.

[43] **The (Worthington) Western Intelligencer**, December 29, 1813, "Frankfurt, Kentucky, Extract of a letter from a volunteer in Captain Dudley's company to a friend at this place, dated Camp Meigs, September 1, (1813)."

[44] Joseph H. Larwill, "Journal of Joseph H. Larwill Relating to Occurences Transpired in the Service of the U States Commencing April 5, 1812," (Unpublished manuscript, Burton Historical Collection, Detroit Public Library), p. 68.

[45] Lindley, **Fort Meigs**, pp. 63-64; Knopf, **The National Intelligencer Reports**, pt. 2, "Chillicothe, Ohio, September 9, 1813," p. 188.

[46] Larwill, "Journal," p. 68.

[47] Knopf, **The National Intelligencer Reports**, pt. 2, "General Orders of Debarkation, of March, and of Battle, September 27, 1813," pp. 245-47; Richard C. Knopf, ed., **Document Transcriptions of The War of 1812 In The Northwest**, Vol. 10, pt.2, **Western Reserve Historical Society War of 1812 Collection**, (Columbus: Ohio Historical Society, 1962), "Harrison's Letter, Delivered On Middle Sister To The Forces About to Invade Canada, September 27, 1813," p. 201; Lindley, **Fort Meigs**, pp. 64-66.

[48] [Chambers?], "The War in Canada."

[49] Knopf, **The National Intelligencer Reports**, pt. 2, "Copy of a letter from Major-General Harrison to the Secretary of War, October 9, 1813," pp. 240-44; "Copy of a letter from Gen. Harrison to the War Department, October 5, 1813," p. 238; Gellner, "Shadrack Byfield," pp. 25-26; Lossing, **Fieldbook**, pp. 553-54.

Conclusion

The War of 1812, perhaps more than any other conflict in American history, has been characterized as one of ambiguity, contradiction and uncertainty. The causes of the war have long been the subject of spirited debate among historians. Although there is general agreement that maritime grievances, agrarian cupidity in the west, and fear of the British/Indian alliance all were contributing factors, the relative importance of each remains undefined and changing as the historiographical controversy continues.

President Madison declared war on Great Britain on June 18, 1812, at a time when England was making a substantial and genuine attempt to resolve the differences between the two nations and avoid conflict. The war was concluded by the Treaty of Ghent, signed on December 24, 1814, and ratified the following February. Under the terms of the agreement the territorial boundaries of the two combatants reverted to the **status quo** of 1811, and the substantiative issues which had led to the war were alreadly ignored. At first glance it appears that the conflict accomplished little in the international arena.

Like the war itself, the contest for the Maumee Rapids is shrouded in ambiguity. That the British twice attacked Fort Meigs and were twice repelled is certain. However, the high numbers of Americans captured and killed after Dudley's

PAINTED BY WOOD   Johnson foremost in his Country's cause.   ENGRAV'D BY C. PHARRISON
The firm supporter of the People's Laws,
While bleeding, struck the desperate blow,
Which laid the mighty chief Tecumseh low.

COL? RICHARD M. JOHNSON

OF KENTUCKY.

*The Victorious Commander of the Kentucky mounted
Volunteers, in the memorable Battle on the banks of the
River Thames, Oct? 5th 1813.*

Richard M. Johnson

Johnson successfully used his military record to further a political career at war's end, rising to the Vice Presidency in 1837. Much of his fame was based on the unverified claim that he had personally killed Tecumseh at the Battle of the Thames. Though Johnson neither confirmed nor denied the story, it nonetheless received wide circulation and, as this 1830's political broadside suggests, did much to enhance his political reputation.

Old Tippecanoe has come out West
William Henry Harrison also used his War of 1812
reputation to further his political ambitions, and was
elected to the Presidency in 1840. In this campaign
broadside from 1840, a grateful Harrison extends the
hand of friendship to an appreciative disabled
veteran, and directs him to a waiting barrel of hard
cider.

disastrous sortie on the north bank during the first siege make any unqualified claim to an American victory in the action tenuous at best. Likewise, the British withdrawal at the conclusion of the second siege can be viewed more as a lack of resolve and a default on Proctor's part rather than the result of American strategic or military superiority.

Ambiguity also seems to define the human scenario, the effects that the experience of service at Fort Meigs brought to those who fought there. To be sure, a few who served at the Rapids were able to capitalize on the experience and profit handsomely from it. William Henry Harrison, for example, used his military record as a springboard into the national political arena, ascending to the Presidency in 1841. Likewise, Richard M. Johnson followed much the same path to the office of Vice President in 1837. Others such as Duncan McArthur and Joseph Larwill would successfully pursue the same strategy to emerge as prominent political leaders on the state and local levels.

But what of the vast majority? What of those who served anonymously and without thought, before or after, of extraordinary recognition or recompense? How did the initial surge of patriotism and national zeal, the catapult of high emotion, sustain them throughout the conflict? The answer is found, in part, in the journal of a young private from Virginia, Alfred M. Lorrain, of the Petersburg Volunteers.

Lorrain had been with his company on the way to the Maumee Rapids when the Petersburg Volunteers marched through Chillicothe, Ohio. Here, the troops were treated to a lavish banquet held in their honor. The largess of the occasion made an indelible impression upon the young boy from Virginia. Awed by the vast array of food and perhaps the ready availability of drink, entranced by cheering crowds, and caught up in the impassioned rhetoric of self-righteous nationalism, Lorrain, reflecting upon the event, wrote in his diary that "Surely, there (is) nothing like the glory and honor of war."

On May 10, 1813, immediately after the first siege had ended, the bodies of the dead were collected from within the fort and the surrounding area and placed in rows just outside one of the gates to await burial the following day. Because of the violent nature of their deaths, many of the victims' bodies were horribly maimed, mutilated and disfigured. Late that evening at about midnight, Lorrain was ordered to stand guard "over this ghastly, silent congregation." Lorrain recalled that:

> As I looked down upon them, I became more astonished at myself than any other part of the creation. I felt truly like an apostate from human nature. A few months before I could not feel comfortable in the idea of sleeping alone. The sight of a corpse could once afford me subject-matter of trembling for weeks to come. Even in the Black Swamp I had a tear to spare to the expiring pack-horse. But now, at this lonely hour, while all the army were wrapped in sleep, except a few widely-scattered sentinels, I could look down on this ghastly, disfigured group, without even a tremor stealing over my nerves. I found that my heart had become wretchedly hardened by the scenes, sufferings, and conflicts of war. What particularly afflicted me was, I thought that all the social feeling and sympathies of my soul were gone forever; that I should no more feel with those who feel, or weep with those who weep.[1]

It was an emotional investment that had led many of these men to the Northwest frontier. Now, that investment was perceived as an expendable commodity to be quickly discarded in the light of the realities of war. Emotional involvement was denied, repressed and abandoned, replaced with a stoic resignation and numbness. Ironically, the contradiction is not surprising when viewed against the ambiguity surrounding Fort Meigs during the War of 1812.

Notes

[1] Alfred M. Lorrain, **The Helm, The Sword, and The Cross: A Life Narrative**, (Cincinnati: Poe & Hitchcock, 1862), pp. 106, 145-46; see also Harlow Lindley, ed., **Fort Meigs and the War of 1812, Orderly Book of Cushing's Company 2nd U. S. Artillery April, 1813 - February, 1814 and Personal Diary of Captain Daniel Cushing October, 1812 - July 1913**, (Columbus: Ohio Historical Society, 1975), p. 119. Cushing writes in the entry for May 9, "The sight of dead men has become no more terrifying than the sight of dead flies on a summer day."

Appendix

At the time of a soldier's death in service, his personal belongings were inventoried and then either returned to his family or sold at auction with the proceeds forwarded to the deceased's estate. These inventories provide a particularly intimate look at the artifacts and material culture associated with a soldier's life on the Northwest frontier during the war. The following inventory is found in a letter from Major George Tod to the Secretary of War, John Armstrong.

****

Inventory of the effects of Captain Asabel Nearing deceased, of the 19th Regiment United States Infantry, who died at Fort Meigs Sept. 10, 1813-----

1 silk sash
1 pair pocket pistols
1 coat
6 shirts
1 full dress coat
4 pair pantaloons
1 pair socks

1 epaulet
2 pair socks
1 waistcoat
1 towel
1 shirt
1 handkerchief, neck
2 silk banded handkerchiefs
1 velvet vest
Smith's Infantry
   Rules & Articles of War &-
1 silver cord & tassel
1 pair leather gloves
1 pure velvet hat ribbon
1 coat
2 oil cloths for a hat
1 pen knife
1 cravat
1 comb
1 flannel coat
1 vest
1 Bible
1 pen knife
1 sword - silver hilt
2 umbrellas - cotton
1 pair shoe brushes
1 pair shoes
1 small bag of black pepper
1 trunk
1 riding whip
1 portable writing desk
2 nutmegs
1 silver watch
2 pair boots
1 hat
1 dirk - silver mounted
1 razor strap & soap box
3 old pocket books

Sir -- The articles above mentioned are the only and all the articles which have been delivered to me, as belonging to the estate of Captain Asabel Nearing,

Deceased, of 19th Regt. U. States Infantry.

He died at Fort Meigs on the 10th day of September last . . . the before mentioned articles, the effects of Captain Nearing were delivered over to me by Lieut. Stephinson of the 19th Infantry, who was a Lieut. in Nearing's Company, and I cannot but believe that he has acted in this affair with a strict regard to honesty.

A part of the effects have been sold by me at Detroit, a few articles remain yet to be sold. Of the sales, an accurate account shall be transmitted to the War Department.

This inventory I should have forwarded much sooner had not the movements of the army rendered it almost impossible. I have twice written to the distressed widow. I have forwarded to her some part of the money, which was the property of her husband, and have advised her of the course she must pursue in order to receive the balance. At the same time I notified her that her orders for money should be complied with. Captain Nearing's family, I have reason to believe, is somewhat numerous and not very affluent. Captain Nearing was a brave and reputable officer. His family, on account of his merits deserve, and no doubt will receive the notice due, on such occasions, from the Government, and the department over which you preside. Be good enough, Sir, to instruct me in whatever further is to be done.

Major George Tod,
19th Infantry[1]

In addition to accounting for the personal belongings of those who had died in service, inventories were often made for personal possessions being shipped for great distances or to document claims for the loss of items destroyed in the service of the United States government. It is interesting to contrast the inventory of Captain Nearing, a company-grade officer, with this inventory of the belongings of Green Clay, Brigadier

General of the Kentucky Militia.

"List of articles for camp, carried to the Northwestern frontier by General Green Clay"

Trunk, portmanteau and fixtures, flatiron, coffee-mill, razor strop, box, etc., inkstand and bundle of quills, ream of paper, three halters, shoe-brushes, blacking, saddle and bridle, tortoise-shell comb and case, box of mercurial ointment, silver spoon, mattress and pillow, three blankets, three sheets, two towels, linen for a cot, two volumes of **McKenzie's Travels**, two maps, spy-glass, gold watch, brace of silver mounted pistols, umbrella, sword, two pairs of spurs, one of silver. Clothes: Hat, one pair of shoes, one pair of boots, regimental coat, great coat, bottle-green coat, scarlet waistcoat, striped jeans waistcoat, blue cassimere and buff cassimere waistcoat, two pair cotton colored pantaloons, one pair bottle-green pantaloons, one pair queencord pantaloons, one pair buff short breeches, one pair red flannel drawers, one red flannel waistcoat, red flannel shirt, five white linen shirts, two check shirts, nine cravats, six chamois, two pair thread stockings, three pair of thread socks, hunting shirt, one pair of leather gloves, one pair of woolen gloves.[2]

[1] National Archives, (Microfilm, M-221, Roll 57, T173).

[2] Anderson Quisenberry, **Kentucky In The War of 1812**, (Baltimore: Genealogical Publishing Company, 1969), p. 52.

Bibliography

Au, Dennis M. **War On The Raisin: A Narrative Account of the War of 1812 in the River Raisin Settlement, Michigan Territory**. Monroe: Monroe County Historical Commission, 1981.

Averill, James P. **Fort Meigs, A Condensed History of the Most Important Military Point in the Northwest, Together With Scenes and Incidents connected with the Sieges of 1813, and a Minute Description of the Old Fort and its Surroundings as they now Appear**. Toledo: Blade Printing and Paper Company, 1886.

Banta, R. E. ed. "A Short Summary of A Journey Taken by Volunteers from Gallia County for the Purpose of Destroying Indians and the Invasion of Canada by Nathan Newsom of Gallia County, Ohio, 1812." Ohio Historical Society.

Bird, Harrison. **War for the West 1790-1813**. New York: Oxford University Press, 1969.

Boehm, Robert B. and Buchman, Randall L., eds. **Journal of the Northwestern Campaign of 1812-1813 Under Major-General Wm. H. Harrison by Bvt. Lieut.-Colonel Eleazer D. Wood, Captain Corps of Engineers, U. S. Army**. Defiance: The Defiance College Press, 1975.

Brannon, John. **Official Letters of the Military and Naval Officers of the United States During the War with Great Britain in the Years 1812, 1813, 1814, and 1815**. Washington: Way and Gideon, 1823.

Brown, Samuel R. **Views of the Campaigns of the North-Western Army**. Burlington, Vermont: Samuel Mills, 1814.

_____ **Views of Lake Erie**. Troy, New York: Francis Adancourt, 1814.

Coffin, William F. "Squire Reynold's Narrative," **1812; The War, and Its Moral: A Canadian Chronicle**. Montreal: John Lovell, 1864.

Coles, Harry L. **The War of 1812**. Chicago & London: The University of Chicago Press, 1965.

Combs, Leslie. **Col. Wm. Dudley's Defeat Opposite Fort Meigs, May 5, 1813, Official Report From Captain Leslie Combs to General Green Clay, Printed for William Dodge**. Cincinnati: Spiller & Gates, Printers, 1869.

"Copies of Letters to and from James Y. Love, Written During the War of 1812." The Filson Club.

Cullum, George W. **Campaigns of the War of 1812-15 Against Great Britain, Sketched and Criticized; with Brief Biographies of the American Engineers**. New York: James Miller, 1879.

Draper, Lyman C., ed. "Witherell's Reminiscences," **Collections of The State Historical Society of Wisconsin, Vol. III**. Madison: The State Historical Society of Wisconsin, 1904.

Esary, Logan, ed. **Messages and Letters of William Henry Harrison, Vol. 2**. Indianapolis: Indiana Historical Commission, 1922-1964.

Forester, C. S. **The Age of Fighting Sail, The Story of the Naval War of 1812**. Garden City, N.Y.: Doubleday & Company, Inc., 1956.

Gellner, John, ed. "A Common Soldier's Account, Shadrack Byfield, a Private in the 41st Foot, Fights Humbly, Patiently, and Bravely, From Detroit to Lundy's Lane." **Recollections of the War of 1812, Canadian Heritage Series, Vol. 4** . Toronto: Baxter Publishing Company, 1964.

Gilpin, Alec R. **The War of 1812 In The Old Northwest.** East Lansing: The Michigan State University Press, 1958.

Horseman, Reginald. **The War of 1812.** New York: Alfred A. Knopf, Inc., 1969.

Howe, Henry. **Historical Collections of Ohio in Three Volumes, Vol. III.** Columbus: Henry Howe & Son, 1891.

Knapp, H. S. **History of the Maumee Valley, Commencing with its Occupation by the French in 1680.** Toledo: Knapp, 1877.

Knopf, Richard C., ed. **Document Transcriptions of The War of 1812 In The Northwest, Vol. 1, William Henry Harrison and The War of 1812.** Columbus: Ohio Historical Society, 1956.

_____ **Document Transcriptions of The War of 1812 In The Northwest, Vol. 2, Return Jonathon Meigs Jr. and The War of 1812.** Columbus: Ohio Historical Society, 1957.

_____ **Document Transcriptions of The War of 1812 In the Northwest, Vol. 3, Thomas Worthington and The War of 1812.** Columbus: Ohio Historical Society, 1957.

_____ **Document Transcriptions of The War of 1812 In The Northwest, Vol. 4, Anecdotes of the Lake Erie Area.** Columbus: Ohio Historical Society, 1957.

_____ **Document Transcriptions of The War of 1812 In The Northwest, Vol. 5, The National Intelligencer Reports The War of 1812 In The Northwest.** Columbus: Ohio Historical Society, 1958.

_____ **Document Transcriptions of The War of 1812 In The Northwest, Vol. 6, Letters to the Secretary of War 1812 Relating To The War of 1812 In The Northwest.** Columbus: Ohio Historical Society, 1959.

_____ Document Transcriptions of The War of 1812 In The Northwest, Vol. 7, Letters to the Secretary of War 1813 Relating To The War of 1812 In The Northwest. Columbus: Ohio Historical Society, 1961.

_____ Document Transcriptions of The War of 1812 In The Northwest, Vol. 10, Western Reserve Historical Society War of 1812 Collection. Columbus: Ohio Historical Society, 1962.

Larwill, Joseph H. "Journal of Joseph H. Larwill Relating to Occurences Transpired in the Service of the U States Commencing April 5, 1812." Burton Historical Collection, Detroit Public Library.

Lindley, Harlow, ed. Fort Meigs and the War of 1812, Orderly Book of Cushing's Company, 2nd U. S. Artillery April, 1813 - February, 1814, and Personal Diary of Captain Daniel Cushing October, 1812 - July, 1813. Columbus: Ohio Historical Society, 1975.

Lorrain, Alfred M. The Helm, The Sword, and The Cross: A Life Narrative. Cincinnati: Poe & Hitchcock, 1862.

Lossing, Benson J. The Pictorial Fieldbook of the War of 1812. New York: Harper and Brothers, 1868; reprint ed., Somersworth: New Hampshire Publishing Company, 1976.

McAfee, Robert B. History of the Late War in the Western Country. 1816; reprint ed., Bowling Green: Historical Publications Company, 1919.

McAfee, Captain Robert B. "Company Memorandum Book & Journal of Robt. B. McAfee's Mounted Company in Col. Rh. M. Johnson's Regiment - from May 19, 1813 inclusive including Orders Issued on the expedition." Robert B. McAfee Papers, The Filson Club.

[McNeal, Robert.] "A Diary of a member of the Pittsburgh Blues, containing an account of the fighting of early companies of men against the Indians and the British throughout this part of Ohio." Yale University Library Manuscripts Collection.

Michigan Pioneer and Historical Collections in 40 Volumes, Vol. 15. Lansing, 1890.

Narrative of the Life of General Leslie Combs; Embracing Incidents In The History of the War of 1812. Washington: American Whig Review Office, 1852.

"Orderly Book of the 5th Regiment of K.V.M. under the Command of Lieut. Col. Com. Will. Lewis, John McCalla, Adjutant." William Lewis Papers, Burton Historical Collection, Detroit Public Library.

Pennsylvania Archives, Second Series, Vol. 12.

Pennsylvania Archives, Sixth Series, Vols. 7, 8, 9, 10.

Pentland, Charles. "Memorandum of the March, Tour, and etc. of the **Pittsburgh Blues** whilst performing a tour of 12 months in the service of the **United States** - taken from a journal kept during the period by Chas. Pentland, a member of the Company." University of Pittsburgh, Darlington Memorial Library, Special Manuscripts Collection.

Quaife, Milo, ed. **The John Askin Papers, Vol. 2, 1796-1820.** Detroit: Detroit Library Commission, 1931.

Quisenberry, Anderson. **Kentucky In The War of 1812.** Baltimore: Genealogical Publishing Company, 1969.

Richardson, John. **Richardson's War of 1812; With notes and a Life of the Author by Alexander Casselman.** Toronto: Historical Publishing Company, 1902.

Simonis, Louis A. **Maumee River 1835 With the William C. Holgate Journal**. Defiance: Defiance County Historical Society, 1979.

Slocum, Charles E. **History of the Maumee River Basin.** Toledo: Brown & Slocum, 1905.

Underwood, Lieutenant Joseph Rogers. "Dudley's Defeat & Running The Gauntlet." The Kentucky Library, Department of Library Special Collections - Manuscripts, Western Kentucky University.

Young, Sally L., ed. "To The Rapids, A Journal of a Tour of Duty in the Northwestern Army Under the Command of Major-General Wm. Henry Harrison, by Sergeant Greenbury Keen, First Regiment, Second Brigade, Pennsylvania Militia." Ohio Historical Society.

Van Tassel, Charles S. **Story of the Maumee Valley, Toledo, and the Sandusky Region**. Chicago: S. G. Clarke Publishing Company, 1929.

Walker, Adam. **A Journal of Two Companies of the 4th Regiment of U. S. Infantry Under Colonel Miller**. Keene, New Hampshire: Sentinel Press, 1816.

———————— "Journal of Adam Walker," **The (New York) Log Cabin,** May 9, 1840.

Wood, William, ed. **Select British Documents of the Canadian War of 1812, in three Volumes, Vol. II**. Toronto: The Champlain Society, 1923.

Wright, Richard J., ed. **The John Hunt Memoirs, Early Years of the Maumee Valley Basin, 1812-1835**. Maumee: Maumee Valley Historical Society, 1979.

Periodicals

Baldwin, C.C. ed. "Campaign of 1813 On The Ohio Frontier, Sortie at Fort Meigs, May, 1813."**Western Reserve Historical Society Tracts** 23 (1874).

Bonner, Capt. James. "Diary of Capt. James Bonner." **Western Reserve Historical Society Tracts** 49 (1879).

Bradley, Glenn D. "Fort Meigs in the War of 1812." **Northwest Ohio Quarterly** 2 (1930).

Christian, Thomas. "Campaign of 1813 on the Ohio River, Sorties at Fort Meigs, May, 1813." **Kentucky Historical Society Register** 67 (1969).

Clift, J. Glen. "War of 1812 Diary of William B. Northcutt." **Kentucky Historical Society Register** 56 (1958).

Compton, H. W. "The Siege of Fort Meigs." **Ohio Archaeological and Historical Quarterly** 10 (1902).

Eubank, James. "The Siege of Fort Meigs." **Kentucky Historical Society Register** 19 (1921).

Green, James A. "Journal of Ensign William Shillenger, A Soldier of the War of 1812." **Ohio Archaeological and Historical Quarterly** 41 (1932).

Hallaman, Emmanuel. "The British Invasions of Ohio - 1813." **Papers on the War of 1812 in the Northwest, No. 1**. Columbus: Anthony Wayne Parkboard & The Ohio State Museum, 1958.

Heflinger, W. M. "The War of 1812 in Northwestern Ohio: The Year of Victory." **Northwest Ohio Quarterly** 23 (1950).

Hoffnagle, Warren Miles. "The Road to Fame: William Henry Harrison and National Policy in the Northwest From Tippecanoe to River Raisin." **Papers on the War of 1812** in the Northwest, No. 6. Columbus: Anthony Wayne Parkboard, 1959.

Niebaum, Captain John H. "The Pittsburgh Blues, The Story of Fort Meigs," **Western Pennsylvania Historical Magazine** 4 (1921).

"Ohio In the War of 1812." **Ohio Archaeological and Historical Quarterly** 28 (1920).

O'Fallon, Colonel. "Siege of Fort Meigs." **Ohio Archaeological and Historical Quarterly** 28 (1920).

Pearkes, G. R. "Detroit & Miami." **Canadian Defense Quarterly** 11 (1934).

Quaife, Milo, ed. "A Diary of the War of 1812." **Mississippi Valley Historical Review** 1 (1914).

_____ "A Narrative of The Northwestern Campaigns of 1813 by Stanton Sholes." **Mississippi Valley Historical Review** 15 (1929).

Quisenberry, A. C. "A Hundred Years Ago, Siege of Fort Meigs and Dudley's Defeat." **Kentucky Historical Society Register** 32 (1913).

Rainwater, P. L., ed. "The Siege of Fort Meigs." **Mississippi Valley Historical Review** 19 (1932).

Saliers, Earl A. "The Siege of Fort Meigs." **Ohio Archaeological and Historical Quarterly** 18 (1909).

Salsich, Neil E. "The Siege of Fort Meigs, Year 1813, An Eye-Witness Account by Colonel Alexander Bourne." **Northwest Ohio Quarterly** 17, pt. 4, & 18 pt. 1 (1945-46).

"Selections from the Gano Papers." **Quarterly Publications of the Historical and Philosophical Society of Ohio** 16 (1921).

Sibert, Daniel. "Daniel Sibert's Reminescences of the War of 1812, Letters to his brother, Jeremiah Sibert." **Kentucky Historical Society Register** 26 (1938).

Slocum, Charles E. "The Origin, Description and Service of Fort Winchester." **Ohio Archaeological and Historical Quarterly** 9 (1901).

Sweeny, Lenora H. "The Pride of Virginia, The Heroes of Fort Meigs." **Virginia Historical Magazine** 47 (1939).

Wallace, Lee Jr. "The Petersburg Volunteers, 1812-1813." **The Virginia Magazine of History** 82 (1979).

Williams, Samuel. "Expedition of Governor Meigs for the Relief of Fort Meigs, 1813." **Ohio Valley Historical Series Miscellanies**, (Cincinnati: Robert Clarke & Company, 1871).

Willson, Samuel Mackay. "Kentucky's Part in The War of 1812, Prologue to Victory, General Orders Fort Meigs to Put-In-Bay April - September, 1813." **The Kentucky Historical Society Register** 60 (1962).

Yost, Robert. "Rob't Yost his Book made for the purpose of noting down our Marching and what we seen and experecit while in the United States service beginning at St. Clearsville Ohio Sept. the third Eighteen hundred and thirteen and continued to note down as we marcht." **Ohio Archaeological and Historical Quarterly** 23 (1925).

Newspapers

Niles Weekly (Baltimore) Register, Vols. 3, 4, 5, & 6 (1812-13).

The (New York) Log Cabin, May 9, 1840.

The (Worthington) Western Intelligencer, December 29, 1813.

Manuscript Repositories

Cincinnati Historical Society
    Miscel. documents
    William Henry Harrison Papers

Detroit Public Library, The Burton Historical Collection
    Green Clay Papers
    Joseph H. Larwill Papers
    Duncan McArthur Papers
    William Lewis Papers

The Filson Club
    Thomas Love Papers
    Robert McAfee Papers

State Historical Society of Wisconsin, Draper Collection
    William Croghan Papers (microfilm)
    William Henry Harrison Papers (microfilm)
    Frontier Wars Papers (microfilm)
    Tecumseh Papers (microfilm)

Toledo and Lucas County Public Library
    Genealogical and Local History Collections

Ohio Historical Society
    Henry Clay Papers
    James Denny Papers
    Larwill Family Papers
    Duncan McArthur Papers (microfilm collection)
    Miscel. Broadside Collection
    Miscel. Military Collection

Parks Canada
    Fort Malden National Historic Park

Public Archives of Canada

The University of Pittsburgh
    Darlington Library Manuscript Special Collections

The University of Virginia
    Joel Leftwich Papers

Western Kentucky University
  The Kentucky Library, Department of Library Special
    Collections-Manuscripts

Yale University
    Yale University Library Manuscripts Collection

Illustration Credits

The following institutions have been most generous in pro-
    viding the source for the illustrations used in this book.
    Their cooperation and assistance is deeply appreciated.

Burton Historical Collection, Detroit Public Library

Buffalo Gazette Extra, August 11, 1813.

William L. Clements Library, University of Michigan

The River Raisin Massacre
Ashbel Walworth Map, Western Basin of Lake Erie,
1813.

Library of Congress, Division of Geography and Maps

William Sebree, Plan of Fort Meigs

Ohio Historical Society

From Benson J. Lossing, **Pictorial Fieldbook of the
War of 1812**, New York: Harp & Brothers, 1868.

Attack on Fort Stephenson
Battle of the Thames
Battle of Tippecanoe
Green Clay
Duncan McArthur
Fort Meigs and Vicinity

Frenchtown
William Hull
The Prophet
Siege of Fort Meigs
Tecumseh

From Library-Archives Collection

Battle of Lake Erie
Battle of the Thames
William Henry Harrison
Colonel R. M. Johnson
Men of Patriotism, Courage, and Enterprise,
July 29, 1812
Mounted Volunteers, September 5, 1812
Old Tippecanoe has come out west

From History Division Collection

Fort Meigs Powder Horn

Parks Canada - Fort Malden National Historic Park

Winchester Humiliated
View of Fort Malden, 1812

State Library of Ohio

From **U.S. 51st Congress, 1st Session, 1889-90. House Documents 1, part 2.**

Map showing the present condition of Fort Meigs, Perrysburg, Ohio, U.S. Army Corps of Engineers, 1888

Toledo - Lucas County Public Library and the Maumee Valley Historical Society

Joseph H. Larwill Map, Camp Meigs and Environs, July 19, 1813
Western Reserve Historical Society, Cleveland, Ohio

Plat Map, Fort Meigs, April 1, 1813

Index

Larry L. Nelson was born in Columbus, Ohio and received his undergraduate and graduate education at The Ohio State University. Since 1976 he has been employed by the Ohio Historical Society where he is currently the administrator at Fort Meigs State Memorial in Perrysburg, Ohio. He is also on the Continuing Education faculty of The Defiance College, the University of Toledo, and Bowling Green State University where he teaches courses in American Decorative Arts. A frequent contributor to scholarly journals, his articles and reviews have appeared in **Ohio History, Antiques Magazine, The Chronicle of the Early American Industries Association,** and **The Journal of the Company of Military Historians.**